Wonderful World of Paper-Pieced Quilt Blocks for Christmas

Dedication

For Coco and Kinley: My why, my heart, and the joy behind every stitch.

Wonderful World of Paper-Pieced Quilt Blocks for Christmas

Landauer Publishing, www.landauerpub.com, is an imprint of Fox Chapel Publishing Company, Inc.

Project Team
Editorial Director: Brian Hurley
Acquisitions Editor: Amelia Johanson
Editor: Sherry Vitolo
Designer: Wendy Reynolds
Indexer: Jean Bissell

ISBN 978-1-63981-159-5

Library of Congress Control Number: 2026937502

To learn more about the other great books from Fox Chapel Publishing, or to find a retailer near you, call toll-free at 800-457-9112 or visit us at *www.FoxChapelPublishing.com.*

We are always looking for talented authors.
To submit an idea, please send a brief inquiry to
acquisitions@foxchapelpublishing.com.

Or write to:
Fox Chapel Publishing
903 Square Street
Mount Joy, PA 17552

Note to Professional Copy Services:
The publisher grants you permission to make up to six copies of any patterns in this book for any customer who purchased this book and states the copies are for personal use.

Printed in China
First printing

Wonderful World of Paper-Pieced Quilt Blocks for Christmas

13 Holiday-Inspired Designs and Festive Sampler Projects

Liza Taylor

Landauer Publishing

Welcome to Holiday Crafting with FPP

I'm so glad you're here! My name is Liza Taylor. I'm a quilt pattern designer from Salt Lake City, Utah, and a mama to two sweet daughters. I began designing patterns in 2021 after having my first daughter, during a season of life where time felt both precious and fleeting. I found myself drawn to creating small, beautiful projects during nap time, pieces that could be finished in short pockets of time but would still feel deeply satisfying. That season is what led me to foundation paper piecing, and I quickly fell in love with its ability to turn even the tiniest moments into something meaningful and creative.

Foundation paper piecing has become such a joyful part of my life, and I love sharing it with others. It allows us to slow down, focus our hands and hearts, and create something special, whether that's a gift for someone we love, a decoration for our home, or simply a project that brings us a sense of calm and accomplishment. This book is all about combining the magic of the holidays with the delight of foundation paper piecing. Inside, you'll find 13 festive FPP block designs, along with a variety of projects that make it easy to stitch your blocks straight into something useful and beautiful. From pillows and table runners to stockings and reusable gift tags, you'll have plenty of ways to bring handmade charm into your celebrations.

One of the best parts of holiday sewing is that it's never just about fabric and thread, it's about creating memories. My hope for this book is that it feels like an invitation. An invitation to carve out a little creative time during a busy season, to make beautiful holiday pieces that feel personal and heartfelt, and to experience the joy that comes from handmade traditions. Whether you're sewing for yourself, your home, or the people you love, I hope these projects fill your holidays with warmth, color, and the simple magic of making.

So, gather your scraps, pick your favorite fabrics, and let's make something festive together. I can't wait to see how you make these blocks your own and infuse them with your creativity.

How to Use This Book

Each block design includes step-by-step assembly instructions and a template. You can make single blocks to use in one of the smaller projects or sew together multiple blocks to create a larger quilt, table runner, or wall hanging—the choice is yours! I encourage you to mix and match the blocks with your favorite fabrics to make each project feel truly personal.

When you're ready to sew, start by choosing a block that excites you. Flip to the project section to see suggestions for how to use it, then gather your fabrics and follow the instructions. If you're new to foundation paper piecing, you'll find tips and tricks sprinkled throughout each project to help you feel confident as you go.

1/2 TSP 2.5 ML

Contents

Getting Started with Foundation Paper Piecing

Foundation paper piecing (often called FPP) is a quilting technique in which you sew your fabric directly onto a printed paper template. Instead of measuring and cutting perfect shapes ahead of time, the paper acts as your guide, showing you exactly where to stitch and trim. This method makes it easy to achieve precise lines, sharp points, and crisp angles every time.

One of the things I love most about FPP is how it takes the stress out of tricky designs. If you've ever struggled to get points to line up just right in traditional piecing (I'm with you!), you'll be amazed at how simple it feels with paper as your guide. Even complex shapes like stars, curves, or intricate holiday motifs come together smoothly because you're following the lines right on the template.

Another wonderful part of this technique is its flexibility. You can use FPP blocks on their own or combine them into larger projects. And because the paper stabilizes the fabric while you sew, it's also a great way to use up smaller fabric scraps that might otherwise feel too fiddly to work with.

Whether you're brand-new to quilting or have been sewing for years, foundation paper piecing opens the door to endless creative possibilities. It's a technique that rewards both patience and playfulness, and once you see how easy it is to get those perfect points, you might just find yourself hooked!

Tools and Materials

Foundation paper piecing mostly uses standard sewing supplies, but it does have a few special requirements. In addition to your sewing machine, you'll need the following tools and materials.

- **FPP Templates**—You will need to copy the templates in this book onto your template paper of choice to make the blocks. Cut them out along the dotted lines and they're ready to use.

- **Template Paper**—The best thing about foundation paper piecing is that you can use several different types of paper, depending on what you prefer. I mostly use regular printer paper as it is budget-friendly and I often have it on hand, but you can also use newsprint or specialty FPP paper. FPP paper is thinner and easier to tear out, but it can be more expensive. This book focuses on traditional foundation paper piecing techniques, so you won't use the template paper options, like freezer paper, that would be used with adhesive-based foundation paper piecing techniques.

- **Thread**—I use the same thread for foundation paper piecing that I use for traditional piecing, and I recommend opting for a good-quality cotton thread. My current favorite is Wonderfil DecoBob 80wt, which creates really flat, crisp seams.

- **Pins**—Any straight sewing pins will do! I like to use the decorative, flat-head pins that can be found in quilting shops or online.

Your usual sewing supplies should work perfectly for foundation paper piecing. Template papers are the only essential tools you might not normally have in your kit.

- **Fabric**—My favorite part of sewing is picking out different fabric combinations. I love to use quilting cotton. Use whatever fabrics you have and love. FPP is great for using up scraps and cut-off pieces.

- **Cutting Mat**—A rotating cutting mat is great for FPP, but not necessary. I also use a standard rectangular cutting mat that doesn't have the rotating feature.

- **Rotary Cutter**—You will need a rotary cutter to trim the fabric to line up with the templates once you've finished piecing everything together. I am obsessed with my OLFA® ergonomic rotary cutter. It fits in my hand well and the blades stay sharp for a long time.

- **Fabric and Embroidery Scissors**—Good fabric scissors and detail scissors are key to any type of sewing! They will save you so much time and headaches, helping you to quickly cut straight, even lines every time. I have had my Fiskars fabric scissors for years and have never had to sharpen them.

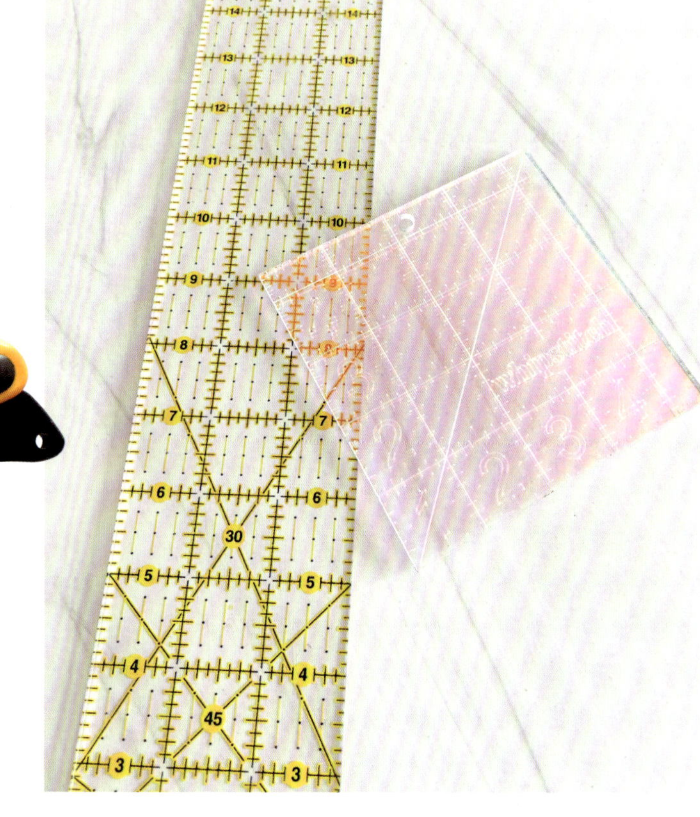

- **Quilting Ruler**—You can use any rulers you might already have. I have a range of sizes and use them all for different projects. I really like my Add-A-Quarter ruler for precision cutting; it has a handy ledge that makes it super easy to cut your seam allowances.

- **Iron**—Any iron will work for foundation paper piecing, but you'll definitely want one with a steam setting. I always finger press and use a seam roller while working to keep the paper from stretching or warping. Once I finish a block, I press it with the iron.

- **Light Box**—A light box or even a bright window is your best friend. Holding your template and fabric up to the light will help you see exactly where your fabric will land. It's one of my favorite tricks for avoiding surprises later!

- **Seam Roller**—If I had to pick one tool as my favorite, it would be my seam roller for sure! I refuse to do FPP without one. Seam rollers are inexpensive, and they'll save you from having to go back and forth to your iron.

How to Foundation Paper Piece

The following steps apply generally to all foundation paper-pieced blocks. Combine these instructions with the templates in this book to create your own projects.

Before You Begin

Choose and cut your fabrics. Each section of the patterns is numbered and colored, so pick fabrics for each section. In general, I recommend trimming your piece at least ½" (1.3cm) larger than the section you are using it for. Often, the hardest part for beginners is cutting the right size of fabric for a section. If you are worried, start by cutting your pieces bigger than you think you'll need. You can always trim your pieces and use the scraps for other sections later on.

Save those scraps. Don't toss your trimmings just yet (even when trimming seams)! FPP is the perfect craft for using up all those little leftover pieces. I'm always amazed at how often a "too small to keep" fabric scrap ends up being just the right fit for a tiny section.

Set your sewing machine stitch length. Because FPP involves sewing the fabric onto the paper and then removing the papers, you need to shorten your stitch length on your machine to make tearing out the papers easier. I always go with a stitch length of 1.5–1.8.

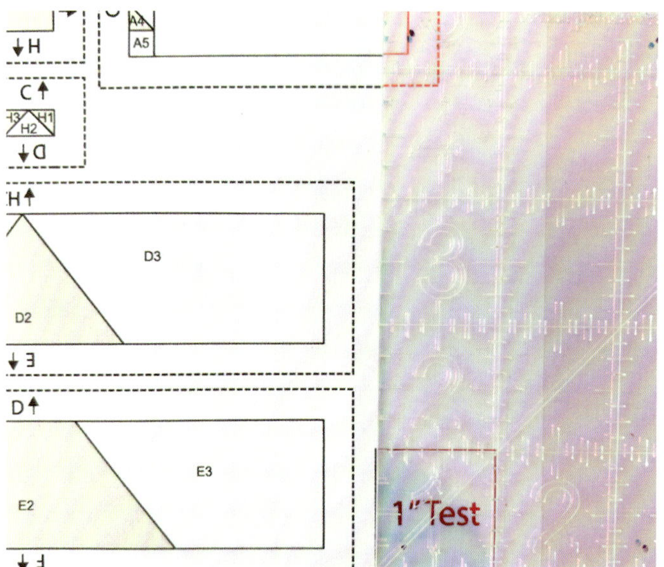

1. Print your template, then measure the 1" (2.5cm) test block on your printed template to make sure it has printed to the correct size.

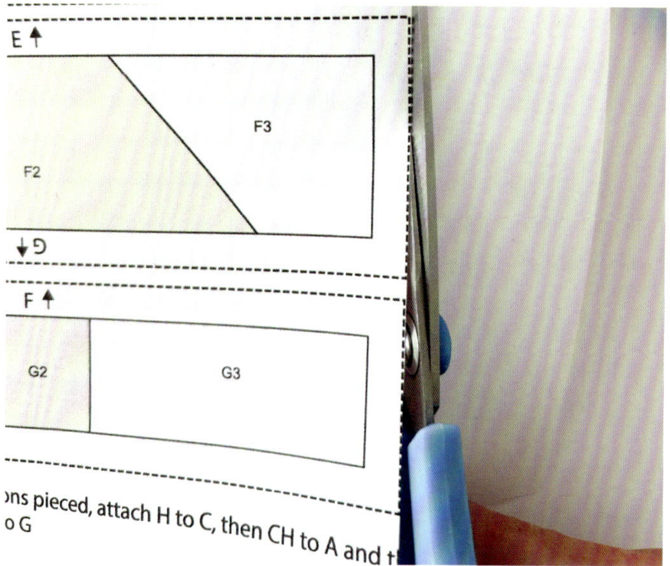

2. Cut each piece of the template out along the dotted lines.

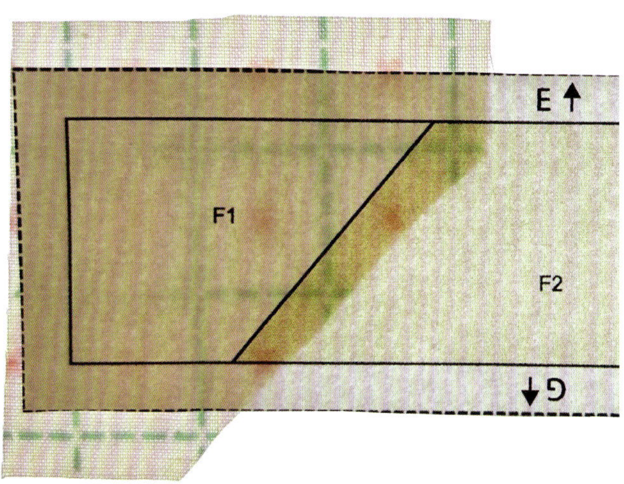

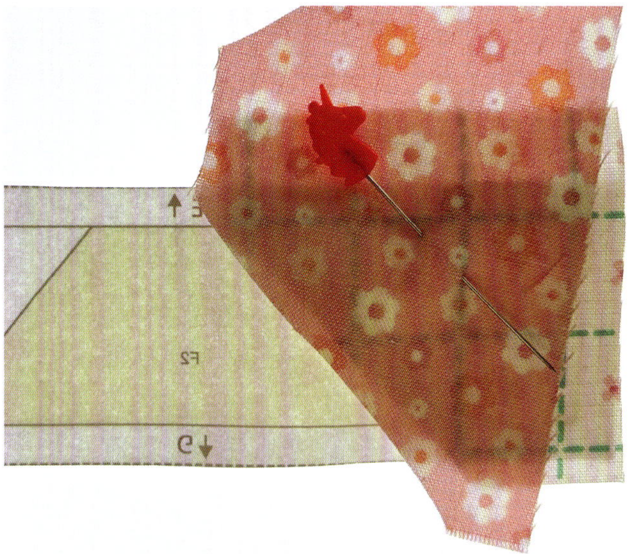

3. Place your template face down (I am working on top of a light board). Place your first fabric piece face up on top of section number 1, making sure it overlaps the surrounding sections by at least ¼" (6.4mm). *Note: In the example picture, I've flipped the paper face up to more clearly show this overlap.* Pin the fabric in place or hold it tightly so it doesn't move.

4. Place your second fabric piece right sides together with the first fabric, making sure the second fabric overlaps the line between sections 1 and 2 by at least ¼" (6.4mm). Pin it in place.

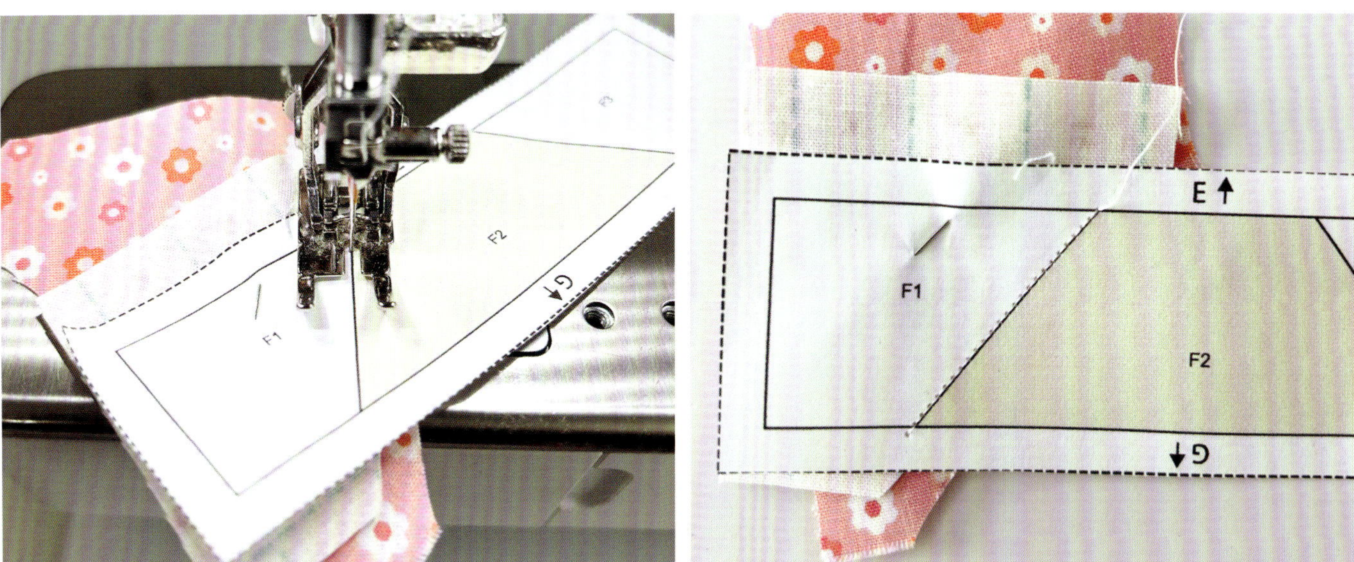

5. Flip over the pinned-together fabric and template so that the printed template is face up. Sew along the solid line between sections 1 and 2. Backstitch at the beginning and the end to reinforce the stitch line.

6. Lay the sewn piece down flat with the printed template right side up. Unpin the fabrics and fold back the paper template at the line you just sewed.

7. Measure and trim ¼" (6.4mm) away from that line.

TIP: It may seem like an extra step to fold and trim after sewing each seam, but it keeps things neat and easy to assemble.

8. Flip the piece over so that the fabrics are right side up. Either iron the fabric or use a seam roller to open the seam and make it lay flat.

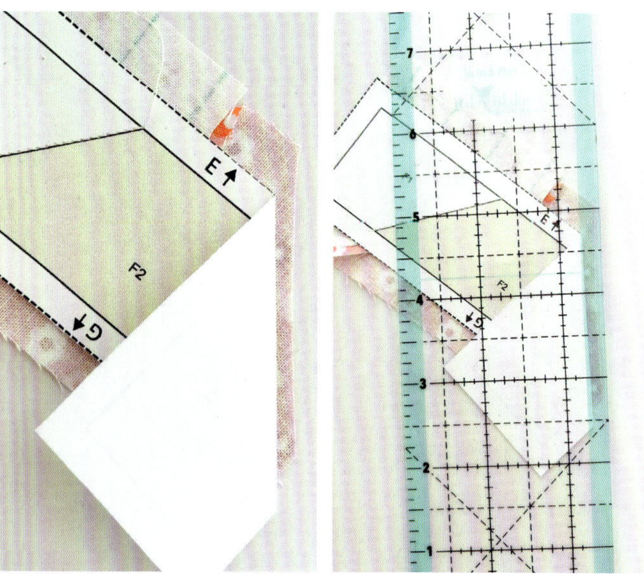

9. Flip the piece back over and fold the template back along the line between sections 1, 2, and 3. If needed, trim ¼" (6.4mm) away from that line to get ready to add the next section.

10. Flip the piece over and line up your third fabric piece with the edge you just cut. Pin it in place.

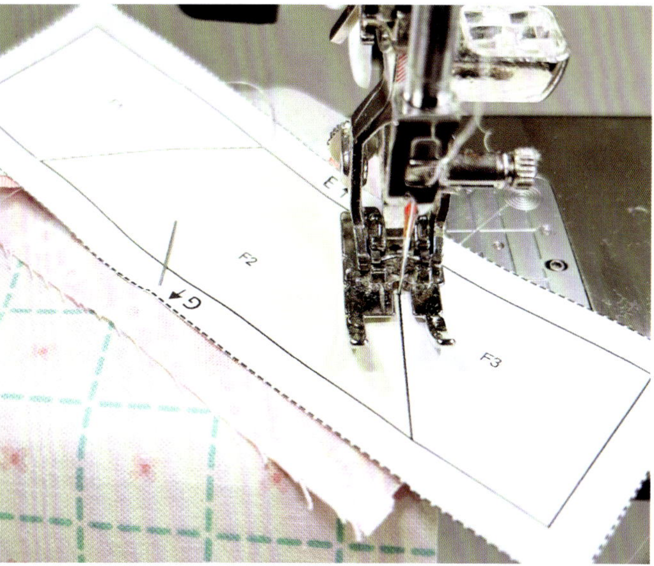

11. Turn the piece over and sew along the solid line between sections 1, 2, and 3. Backstitch at the beginning and the end to reinforce the stitch line.

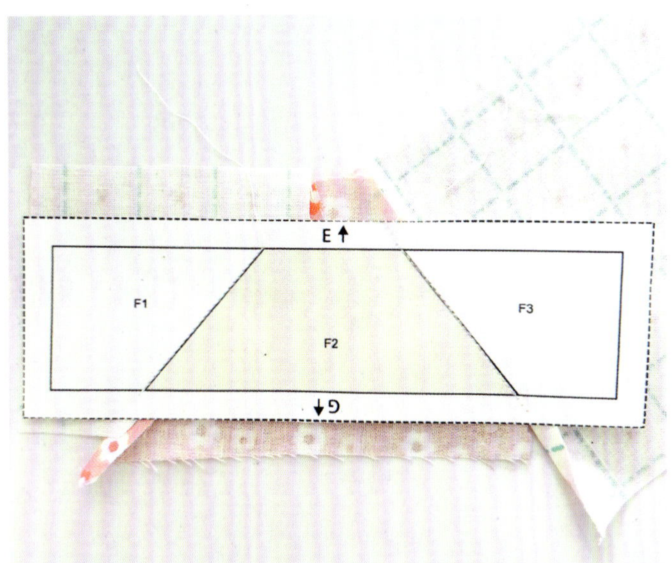

12. Repeat steps 6–8, then flip the piece over, fold the template back along the line between sections 3 and 4. Continue to piece, sew, and trim until all the sections have been added.

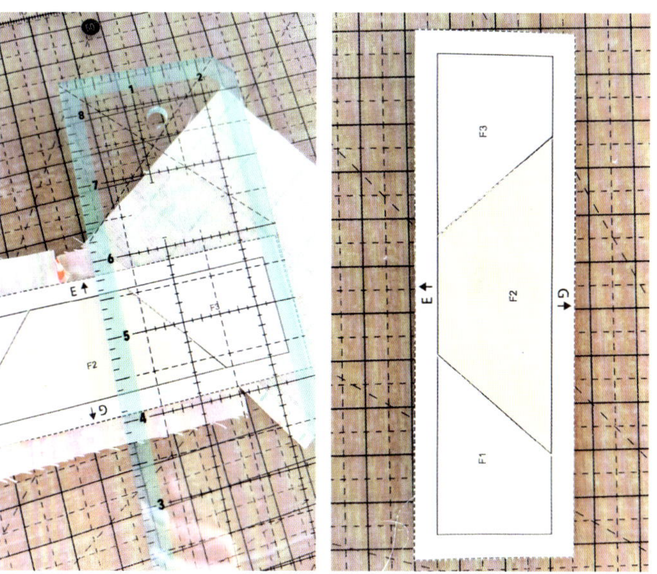

13. Lay the piece on your cutting mat with the printed template facing up. Trim all the fabrics down to the dotted line. Continue with the remaining pieces of the template.

Once all the sections have all been sewn together, you'll have a finished block! Tear away the paper template pieces and give it a good press with your iron and it is all done. You did it!

Tips to Ensure Success

Take your time with angles. Angle seams are sneaky! Always test-fold your fabric before sewing to make sure it fully covers the space. I've learned the hard way that a quick check saves a lot of frustration later.

Stay organized. Keeping your templates and sections grouped makes life so much easier. I like to label everything and set it aside in order, so when it's time to assemble, I'm not searching for the right piece.

Done is better than perfect. Foundation paper piecing is supposed to be fun! If something's a little wonky, chances are you'll be the only one who notices. Once your block is sewn into a project, those tiny imperfections fade away—and all that's left is something beautiful you made with your own two hands.

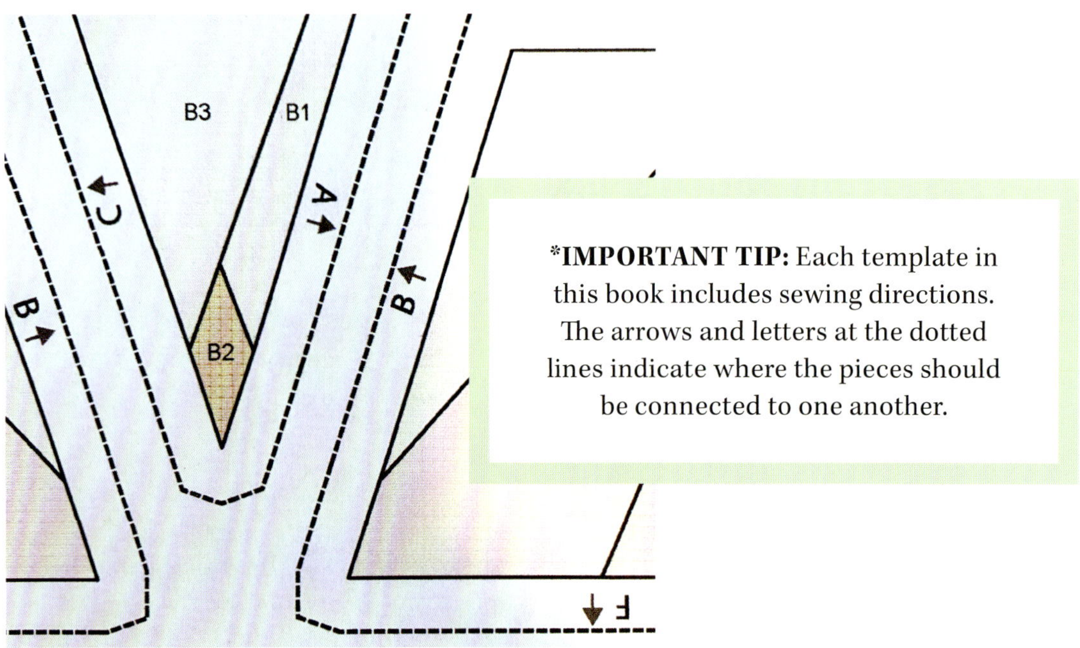

***IMPORTANT TIP:** Each template in this book includes sewing directions. The arrows and letters at the dotted lines indicate where the pieces should be connected to one another.

Resizing the Patterns

The patterns in this book come in two sizes: 5" (12.7cm) and 7" (17.8cm) finished squares. If you have an idea for a project in mind, but you need a block to be bigger or smaller, you're in luck. These patterns are easy to resize at home with just a bit of simple math.

If math isn't your favorite part of quilting, don't worry! I've created a handy chart with several sizes already calculated for you (see below). We will be working in percentages: taking the desired finished size, dividing it by the template's current size, then multiplying this number by 100 to determine the resizing percentage. To use the chart, find the current size of the template on the left side, then find your desired size on the top row. Where the correct column and row meet, you'll find the correct resizing percentage.

Once you know the percentage by which you want to resize the template, enter the percentage in the "scale" box on your printer. The photos here show what my printer's settings look like when I'm printing the template at regular size and at a reduced size. Notice how the preview image (in the top left) shows that the template will be smaller on the page.

Scaling the blocks down is easy: the templates will usually fit on a single 8½" x 11" (21.6 x 27.9cm) sheet of paper. When you scale the blocks up, some templates might be too big to fit on a single standard page. If your enlarged templates must print on multiple pages, cut them out and tape them together to create a single enlarged template.

Template Resizing Percentage Chart

Current Size	Desired Finished Size									
	3" (7.6cm)	**4" (10.2cm)**	**5" (12.7cm)**	**6" (15.2cm)**	**7" (17.8cm)**	**8" (20.3cm)**	**9" (22.9cm)**	**10" (25.4cm)**	**11" (27.9cm)**	**12" (30.5cm)**
5" (12.7cm)	60%	80%	100%	120%	140%	160%	180%	200%	220%	240%
7" (17.8cm)	43%	57%	71%	86%	100%	114%	129%	143%	157%	171%

If your desired finished block size isn't on the percentage chart, use this equation to figure out the percentage by which the template needs to be enlarged or reduced.

$$\frac{\text{Desired Finished Size}}{\text{Current Starting Size}} \times 100 = \text{Resizing Percentage}$$

***IMPORTANT TIP:** When you scale the patterns up or down, the outer seam allowance will also be resized, meaning it will be incorrect as shown on the printed template. You must measure and redraw a ¼" (6.4mm) outer seam allowance around every resized template.

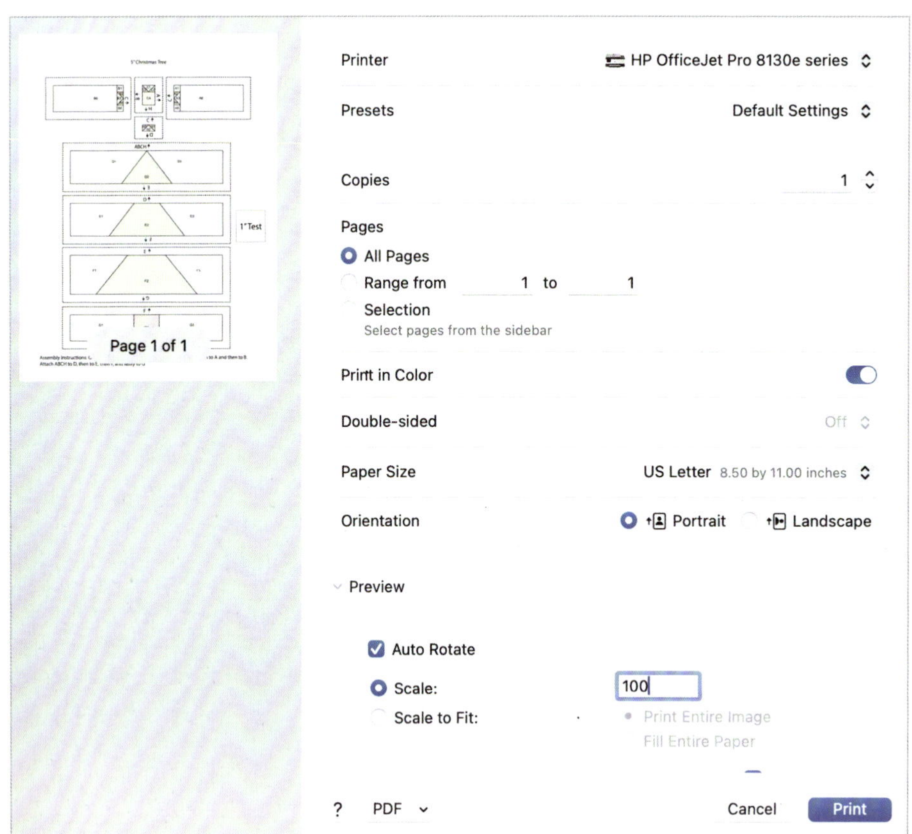

When printing a template at full size, the scale showing on the printer should be set to 100%.

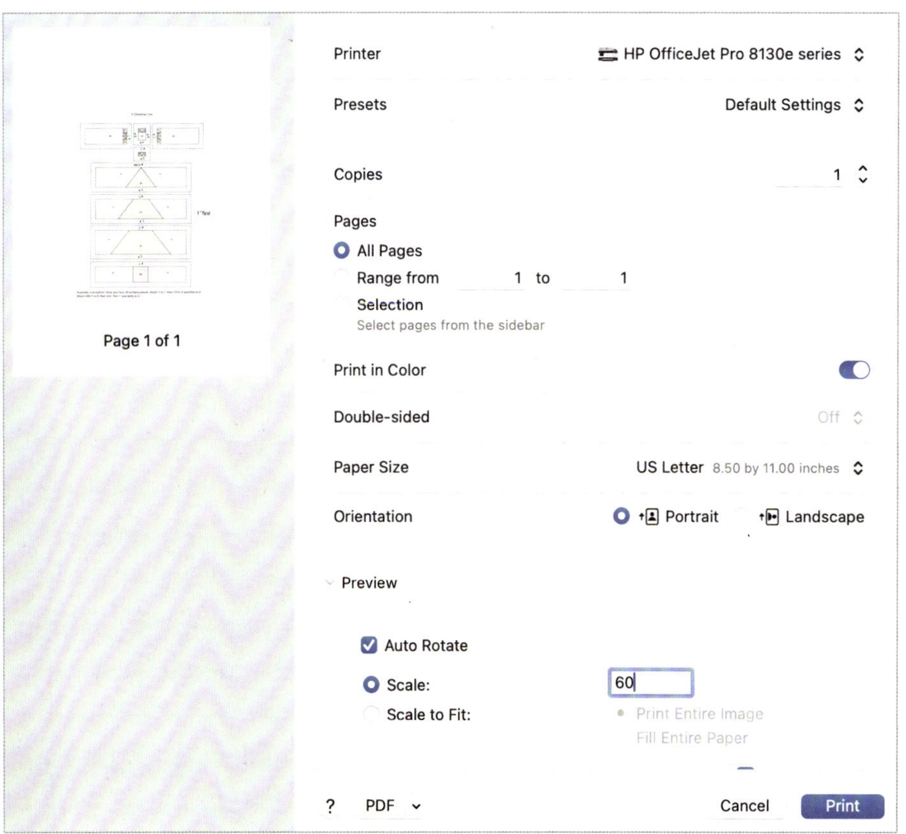

In this case, I want to create a smaller block, so I've scaled the template down to 60%.

The Holiday Block Library

Here you'll find 13 gorgeous holiday block patterns to capture the warmth of the season—from mittens and hot cocoa to reindeer and nutcrackers. The templates are included with the block profiles in this section at the 5" (12.7cm) size and I've included templates in the 7" (17.8cm) size starting on page 92. Both sizes are perfect for the projects starting on page 61. And remember, if you want to make the blocks in different sizes, refer to the Resizing the Patterns section on page 17 for guidance.

***Important Tip:** Remember that each template includes sewing directions. The arrows and letters at the dotted lines indicate where the pieces should be connected to one another.

Winter Star

This star is a joyful design that uses four colors to create a captivating kaleidoscope effect. It's a wonderful opportunity to play with contrast and color placement while creating something truly special for the holidays. This block is a stunning way to add sparkle and movement to your Christmas projects.

Assembly Instructions

1. Once you have all the sections pieced, attach section L to section K.
2. Attach unit KL to section C.
3. Attach section D to section J.
4. Attach unit DJ to section I.
5. Attach unit DIJ to unit CKL.
6. Attach unit CDIJKL to section A.
7. Attach unit ACDIJKL to section B.
8. Attach section G to section H.
9. Attach unit GH to section F.
10. Attach section E to section M.
11. Attach unit EM to section N.
12. Attach unit EMN to unit GHF.
13. Attach unit EGHFMN to unit ABCDIJKL.

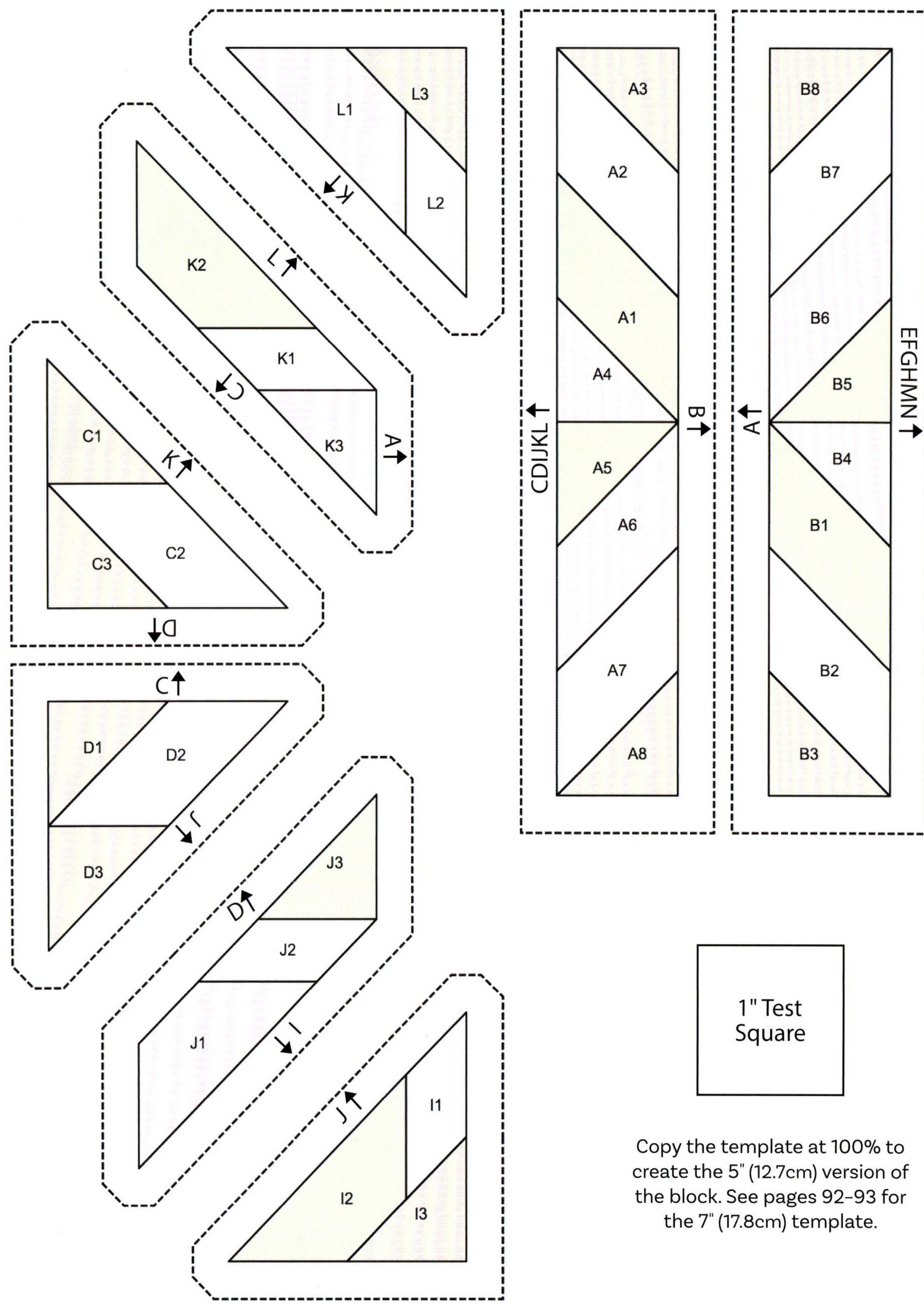

1" Test Square

Copy the template at 100% to create the 5" (12.7cm) version of the block. See pages 92–93 for the 7" (17.8cm) template.

1" Test Square

Copy the template at 100% to create the 5" (12.7cm) version of the block. See pages 92–93 for the 7" (17.8cm) template.

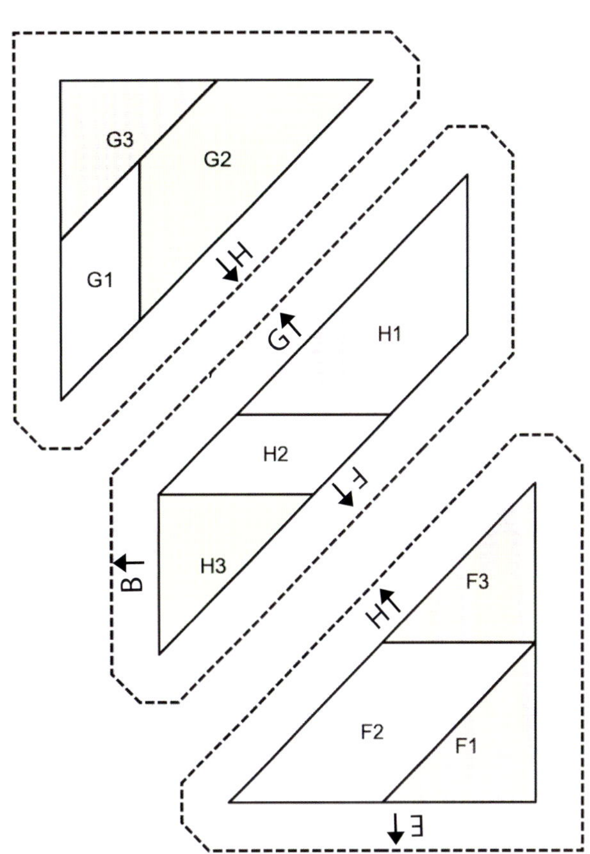

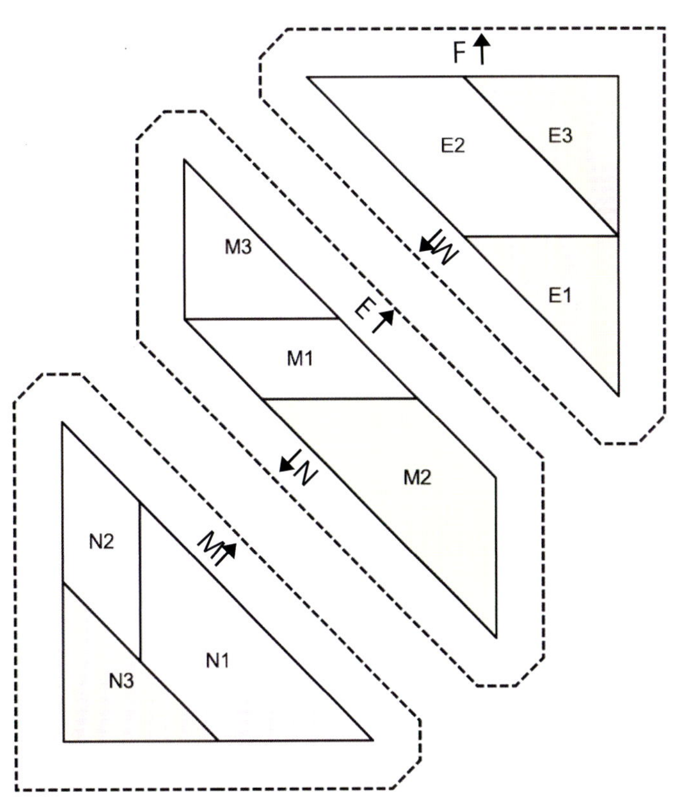

Happy Snowman

Say hello to your new favorite winter friend! This snowman block is playful, festive, and bursting with holiday charm. It's a fun way to add personality to any holiday decorations, making it a delightful project to stitch up during the cozy winter season.

Assembly Instructions

1. Once you have all the sections pieced, attach section B to section C.
2. Attach unit BC to section D.
3. Attach unit BCD to section E.
4. Attach unit BCDE to section A.
5. Attach section F to one side of unit ABCDE.
6. Attach section G to the other side of unit ABCDEF.
7. Attach section J to section I.
8. Attach unit IJ to section H.
9. Attach unit HIJ to section K.
10. Attach unit HIJK to section L.
11. Attach section O to section N.
12. Attach unit NO to section M.
13. Attach unit MNO to unit HIJKL.
14. Attach unit HIJKLMNO to unit ABCDEFG.

The background and snowman colors in the template are very similar. Here is a guide to keep track of your template and fabric pieces.
Background Pieces: A9, A10, D2, E2, F1, G1, H2, H3, I4, J4, K1, L1, M5, M6, M7, O4, O5, O6
Snowman Pieces: A1, A3, A5, A6, B2, B3, C1, D1, E1, I1, J1, M2, M3, M4, N2, N3, O2, O3

1 TBSP 15 ML
1 TSP 5 ML

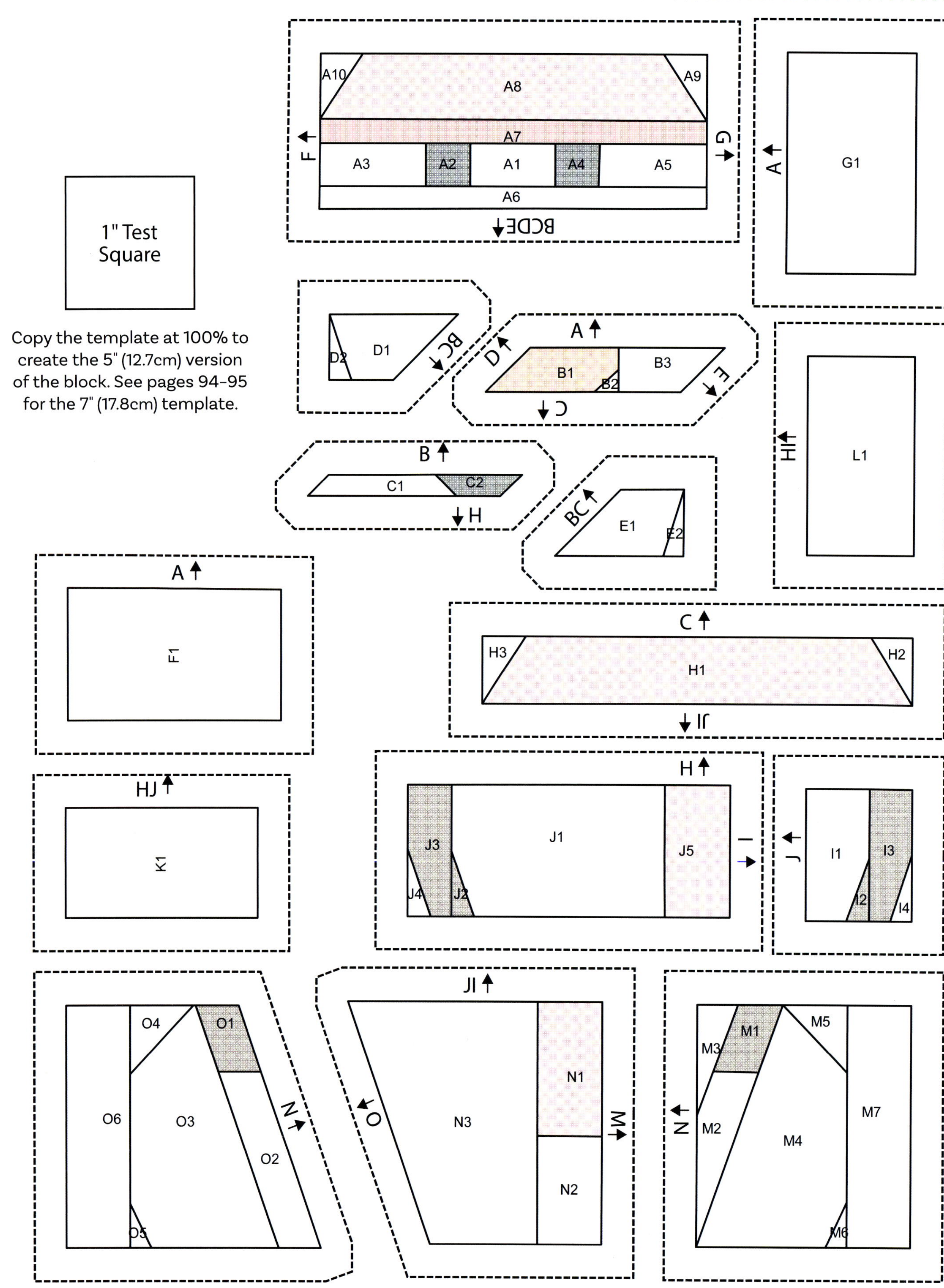

Copy the template at 100% to create the 5" (12.7cm) version of the block. See pages 94–95 for the 7" (17.8cm) template.

Cozy Mittens

This mittens block was designed with fussy cutting in mind. It's a fun opportunity to highlight special prints and add charming details to each glove. You can go classic and cozy or bright and whimsical; either way, this block will bring warmth, creativity, and a whole lot of holiday fun to your sewing.

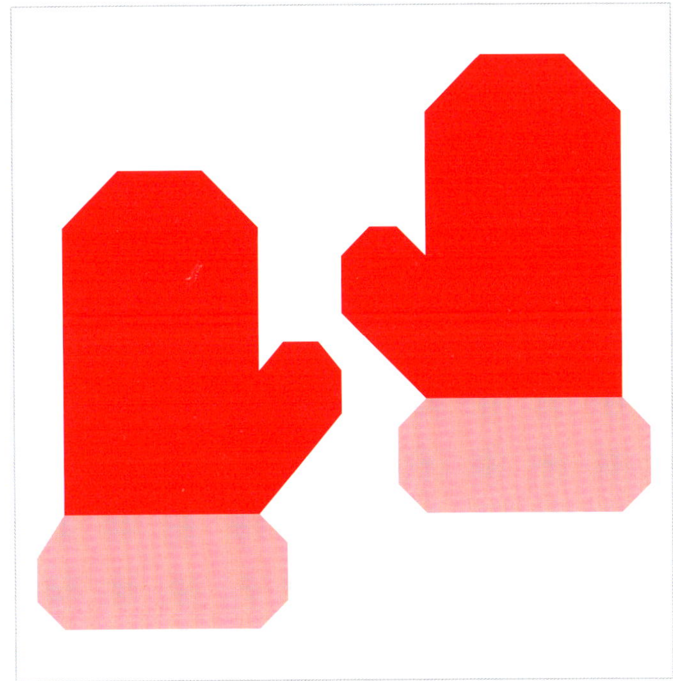

Assembly Instructions

1. Once you have all the sections pieced, attach section A to section B.
2. Attach unit AB to section C.
3. Attach section E to section D.
4. Attach unit DE to section F.
5. Attach unit ABC to unit DEF.

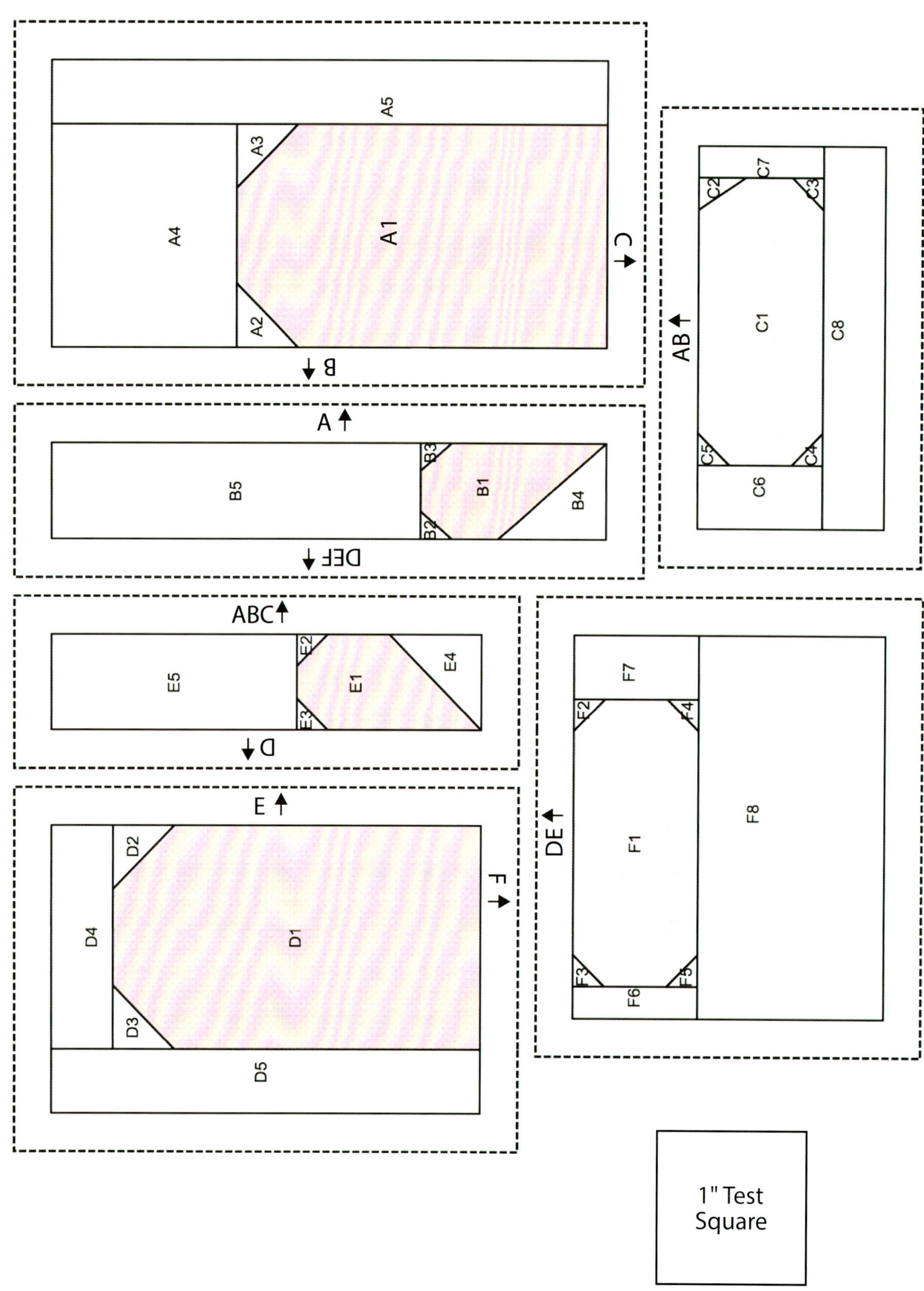

Copy the template at 100% to create the 5" (12.7cm) version of the block. See pages 111–112 for the 7" (17.8cm) template.

1 TBSP 15 ML
1 TSP 5 ML

Hot Cocoa Mug

This hot cocoa mug block captures everything we love about the holidays—warm drinks, cozy spaces, and handmade touches. Sew it into the Warm and Toasty Coasters project on page 81 and customize it to match your favorite mug for a charming, personal detail that brings instant holiday cheer to your home.

Assembly Instructions

1. Once you have all the sections pieced, attach section A to section D.
2. Attach unit AD to section E.
3. Attach unit ADE to section F.
4. Attach unit ADEF to section C.
5. Attach unit ACDEF to section B.
6. Attach unit ABCDEF to section G.

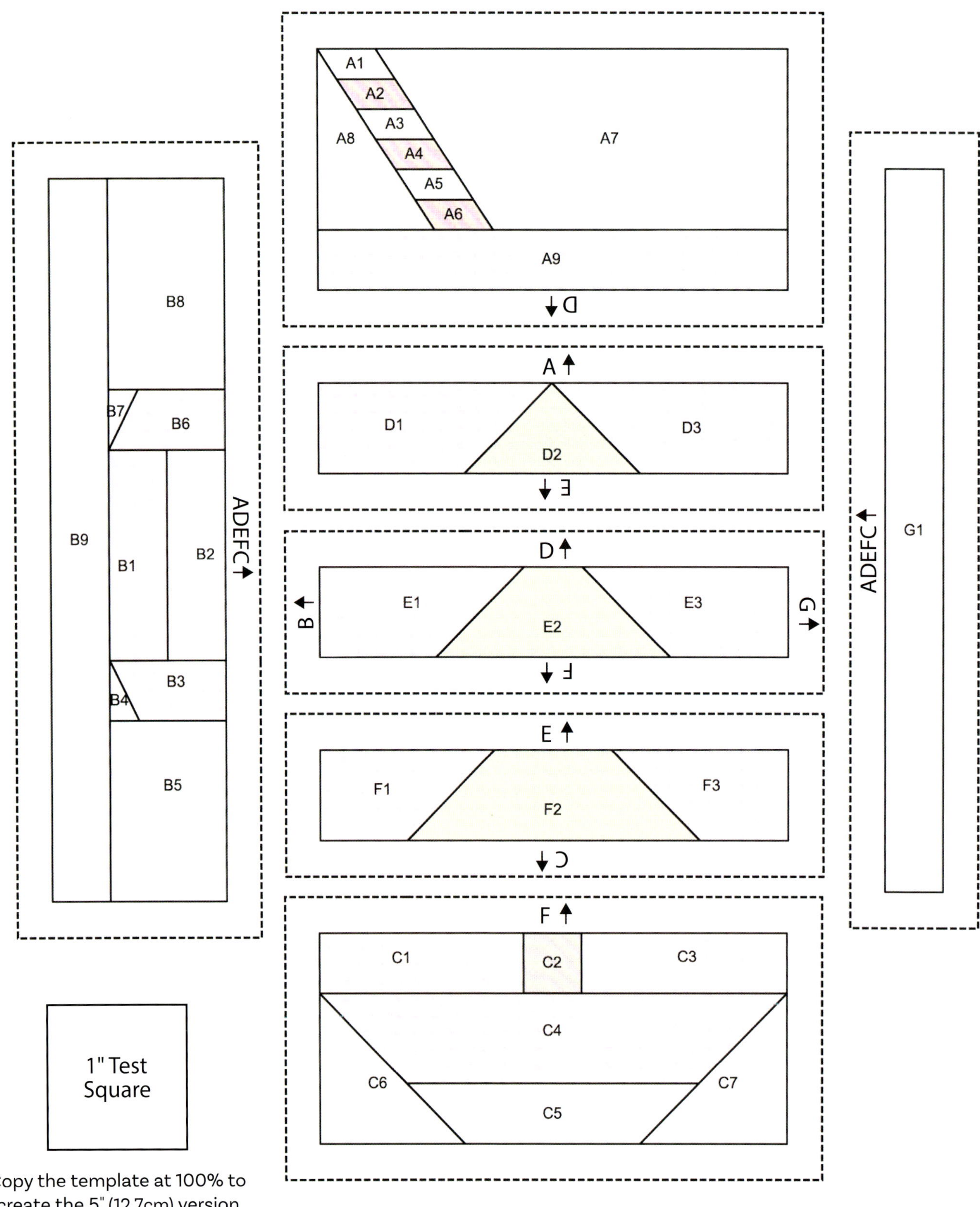

Copy the template at 100% to create the 5" (12.7cm) version of the block. See pages 96–97 for the 7" (17.8cm) template.

Christmas Tree

No Christmas collection would be complete without a Christmas tree! I topped it with a twinkly star on top for extra holiday cheer. I think this is the perfect block to use in the Perfect Oven Mitts project on page 87 to liven up your kitchen all holiday season.

Assembly Instructions

1. Once you have all the sections pieced, attach section H to section C.
2. Attach unit CH to section A.
3. Attach unit ACH to section B.
4. Attach unit ABCH to section D.
5. Attach unit ABCDH to section E.
6. Attach unit ABCDEH to section F.
7. Attach unit ABCDEFH to section G.

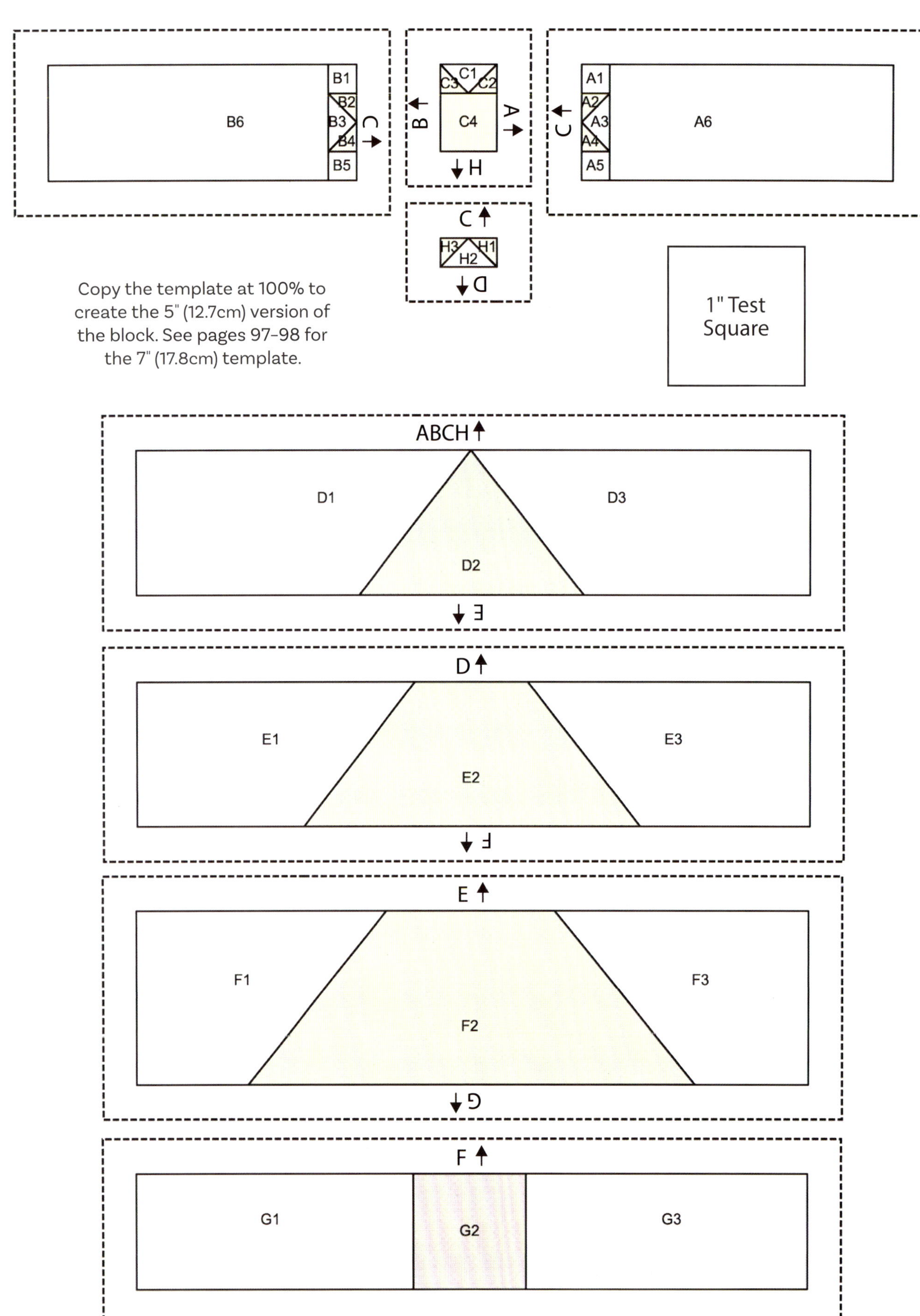

Copy the template at 100% to create the 5" (12.7cm) version of the block. See pages 97–98 for the 7" (17.8cm) template.

1 TBSP 15 ML
1 TSP 5 ML

Santa Hat

Nothing says Christmas quite like a Santa hat! This block is cheerful, classic, and full of holiday spirit. Keep it traditional or give it a modern twist, either way it's a joyful nod to all things merry and bright.

Assembly Instructions

1. Once you have all the sections pieced, attach section B to section C.
2. Attach unit BC to section A.
3. Attach unit ABC to section D.

TIP: Sections A2 and B1 are the folded-over top of the hat. They should be a different shade of red.

1 TBSP 15 ML
1 TSP 5 ML

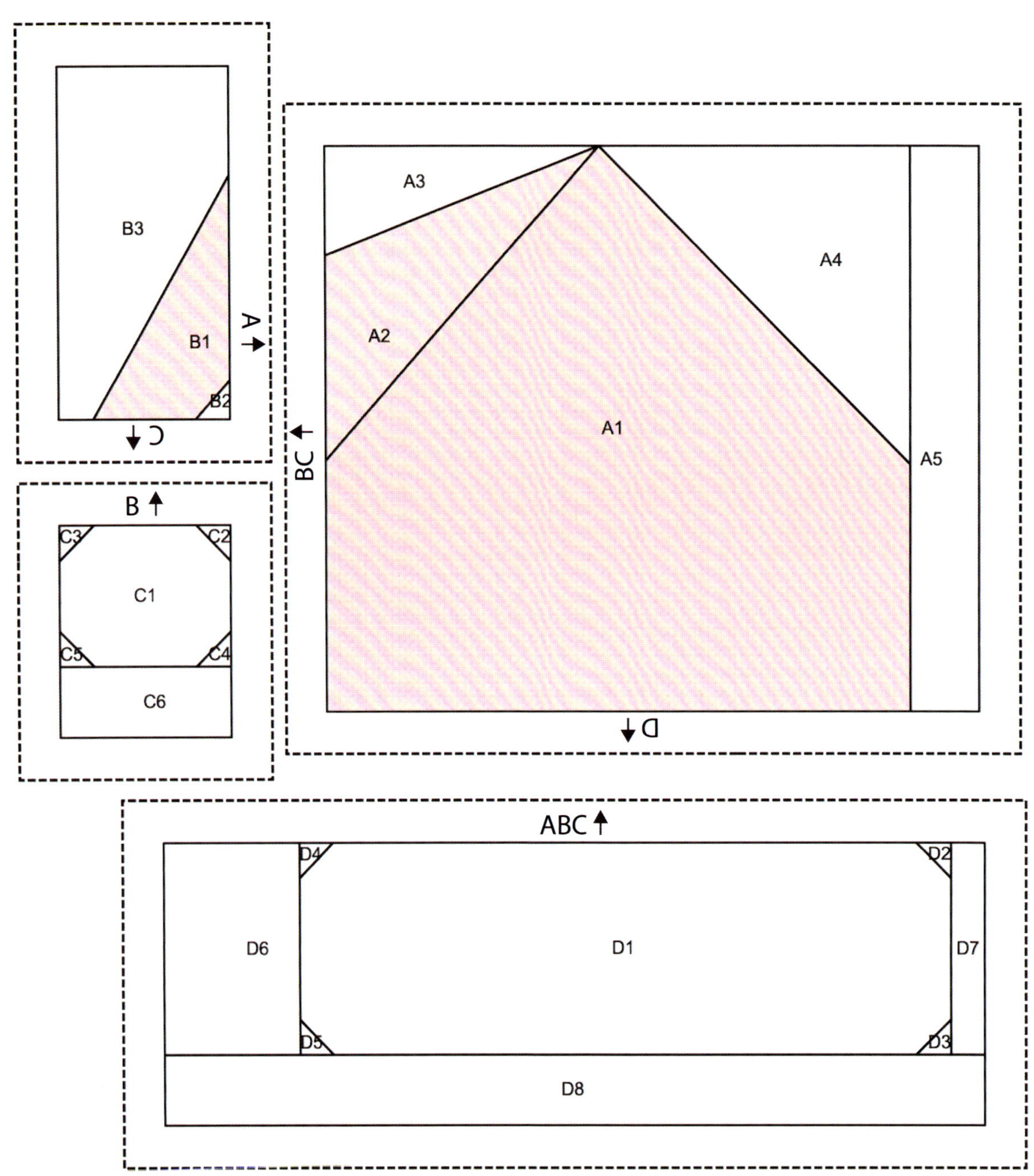

Copy the template at 100% to create the 5" (12.7cm) version of the block. See page 109 for the 7" (17.8cm) template.

1" Test Square

Holly Berries

Holly berries are a true symbol of the season, and this block definitely captures that timeless holiday charm. This block is perfect for making handmade gifts you'll treasure year after year. I used it with the Merry Pillow Covers project on page 74, and the finished piece is perfect for displaying on your couch or coziest chair.

Assembly Instructions

1. Once you have all the sections pieced, attach section A to section B.
2. Attach section C to section I.
3. Attach unit AB to unit CI.
4. Attach section J to section H.
5. Attach unit HJ to section D.
6. Attach unit ABCI to unit DHJ.
7. Attach unit ABCDHIJ to section F.
8. Attach unit ABCDFHIJ to section G.
9. Attach unit ABCDFGHIJ to section E.

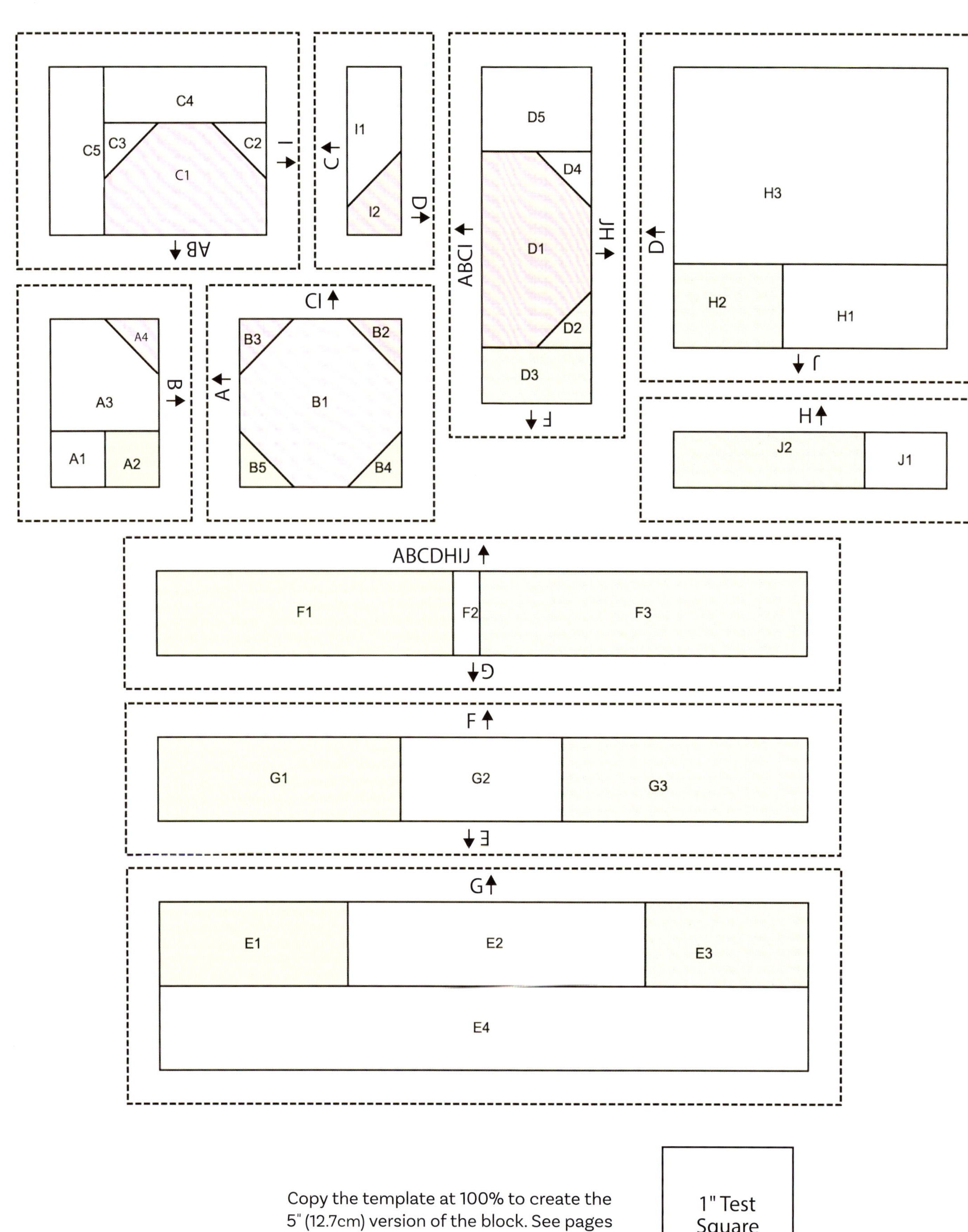

Copy the template at 100% to create the 5" (12.7cm) version of the block. See pages 99–100 for the 7" (17.8cm) template.

1" Test Square

1 TBSP 15 ML
1 TSP 5 ML

Candy Cane

This candy cane block is as versatile as it is festive. Its classic shape and stripes make it a perfect companion for any other block in this book, adding instant holiday charm wherever it goes. Mix, match, and let your creativity run wild!

Assembly Instructions

1. Once you have all the sections pieced, attach section A to section B.
2. Attach unit AB to section C.

1 TBSP 15 ML
1 TSP 5 ML

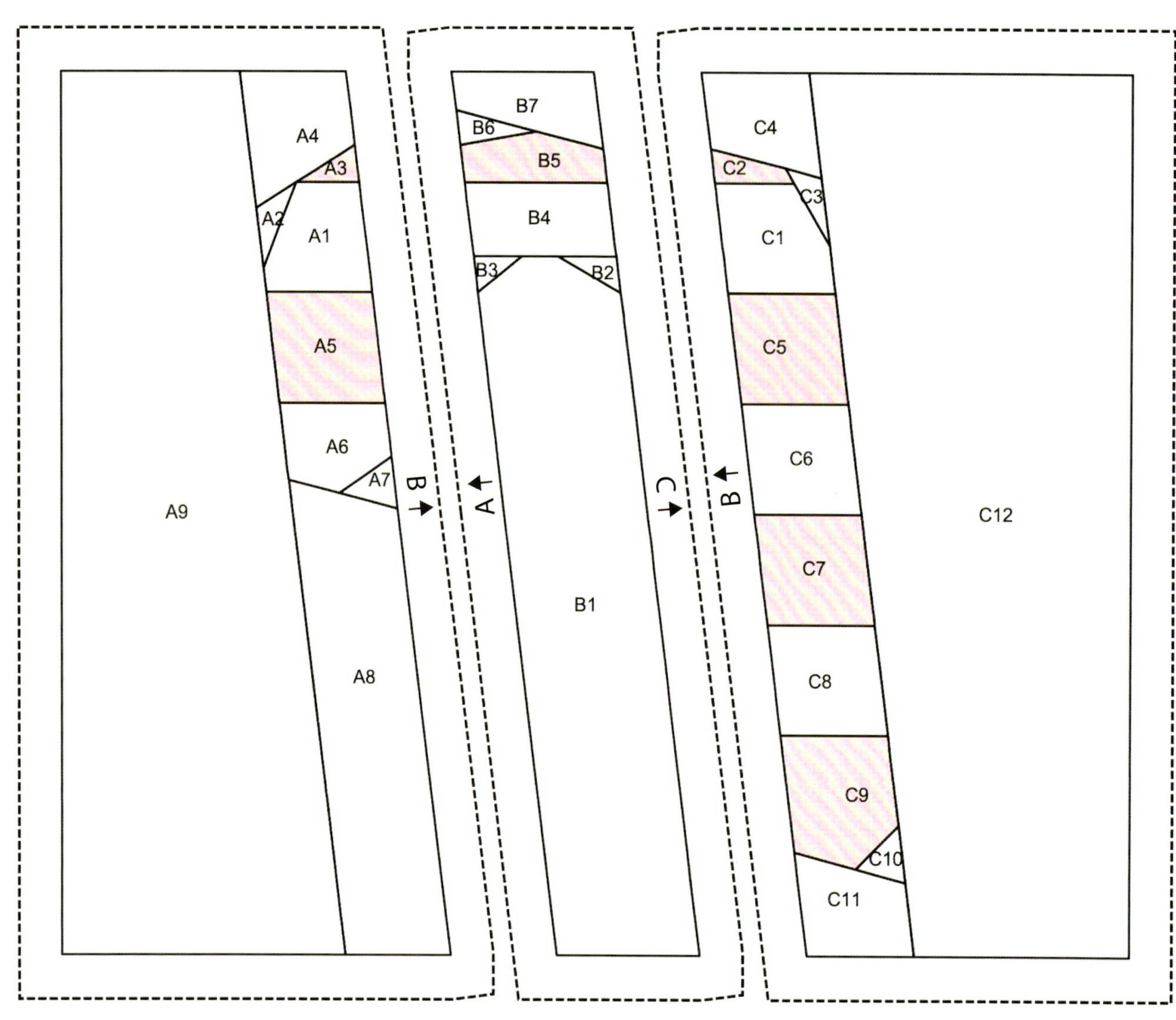

Copy the template at 100% to create the 5" (12.7cm) version of the block. See pages 100–101 for the 7" (17.8cm) template.

1" Test Square

Red-Nosed Reindeer

Meet Rudolph, the reindeer who brings the magic of classic Christmases to your sewing projects! This block reminds us of the nostalgic joys of the season, the sparkle of lights, the excitement in the air, and the timeless charm of everyone's favorite, red-nosed reindeer.

Assembly Instructions

1. Once you have all the sections pieced, attach section A to section B.
2. Attach section C to section D.
3. Attach unit AB to unit CD.
4. Attach section E to section F.
5. Attach unit EF to section G.
6. Attach section H to section I.
7. Attach unit HI to section J.
8. Attach unit ABCD to unit EFG.
9. Attach unit ABCDEFG to unit HIJ.
10. Attach unit ABCDEFGHIJ to section K.

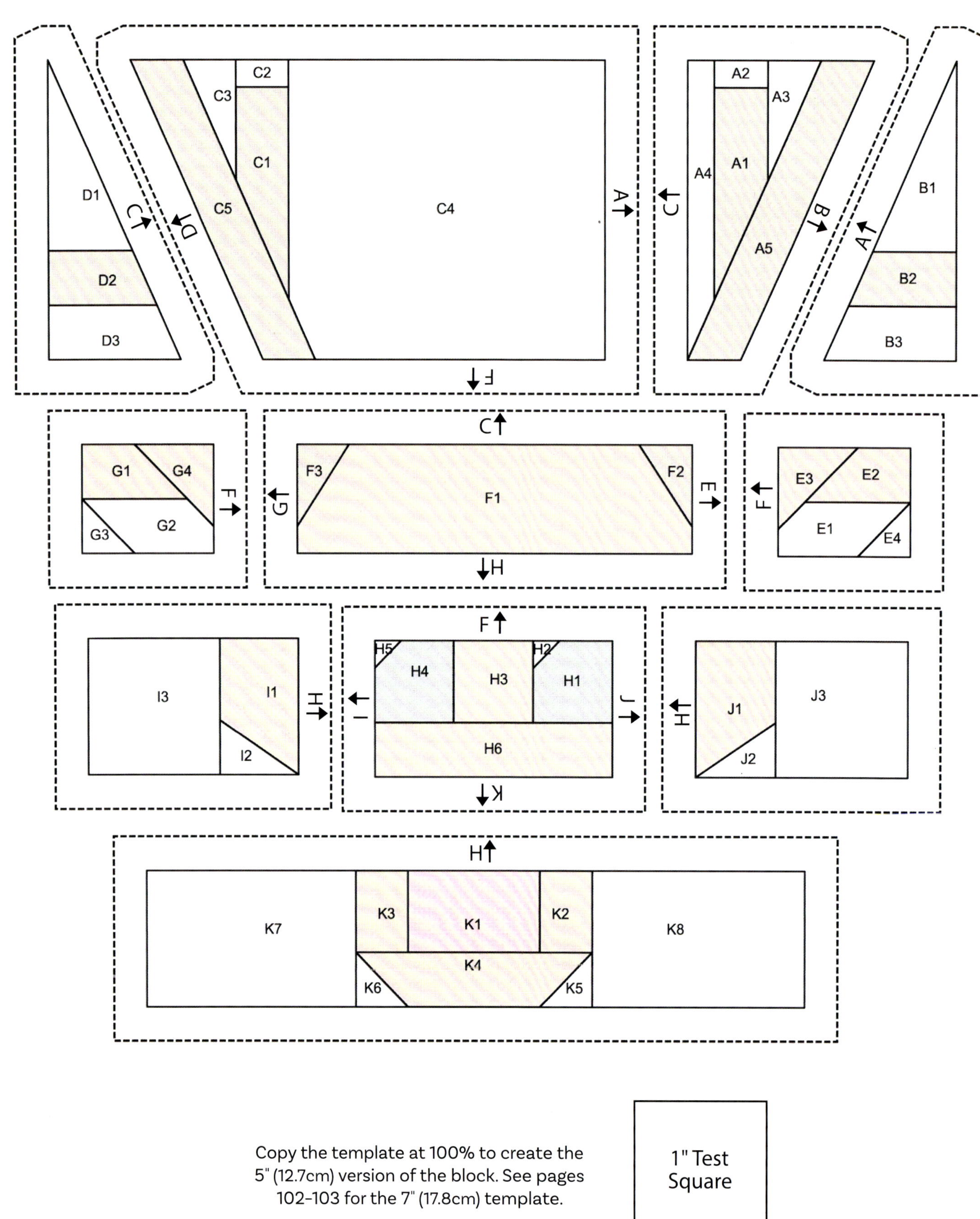

Copy the template at 100% to create the 5" (12.7cm) version of the block. See pages 102–103 for the 7" (17.8cm) template.

1" Test Square

Gingerbread Man

The gingerbread man block is a sweet, cheerful reminder of Christmas in the kitchen—the smell of ginger and spice, warm cookies on the counter, and the joy of making something by hand. This block will bring all those cozy holiday feelings to your projects. Add it to the Festive Hot Pad or Perfect Oven Mitts projects on pages 78 and 87 for a wonderful gift to your favorite baker.

Assembly Instructions

1. Once you have all the sections pieced, attach section A to section C.
2. Attach section D to section B.
3. Attach unit AC to unit BD.
4. Attach unit ABCD to section E.
5. Attach unit ABCDE to section F.
6. Attach unit ABCDEF to section G.
7. Attach section H to section I.
8. Attach unit HI to unit ABCDEFG.

1 TBSP 15 ML
1 TSP 5 ML

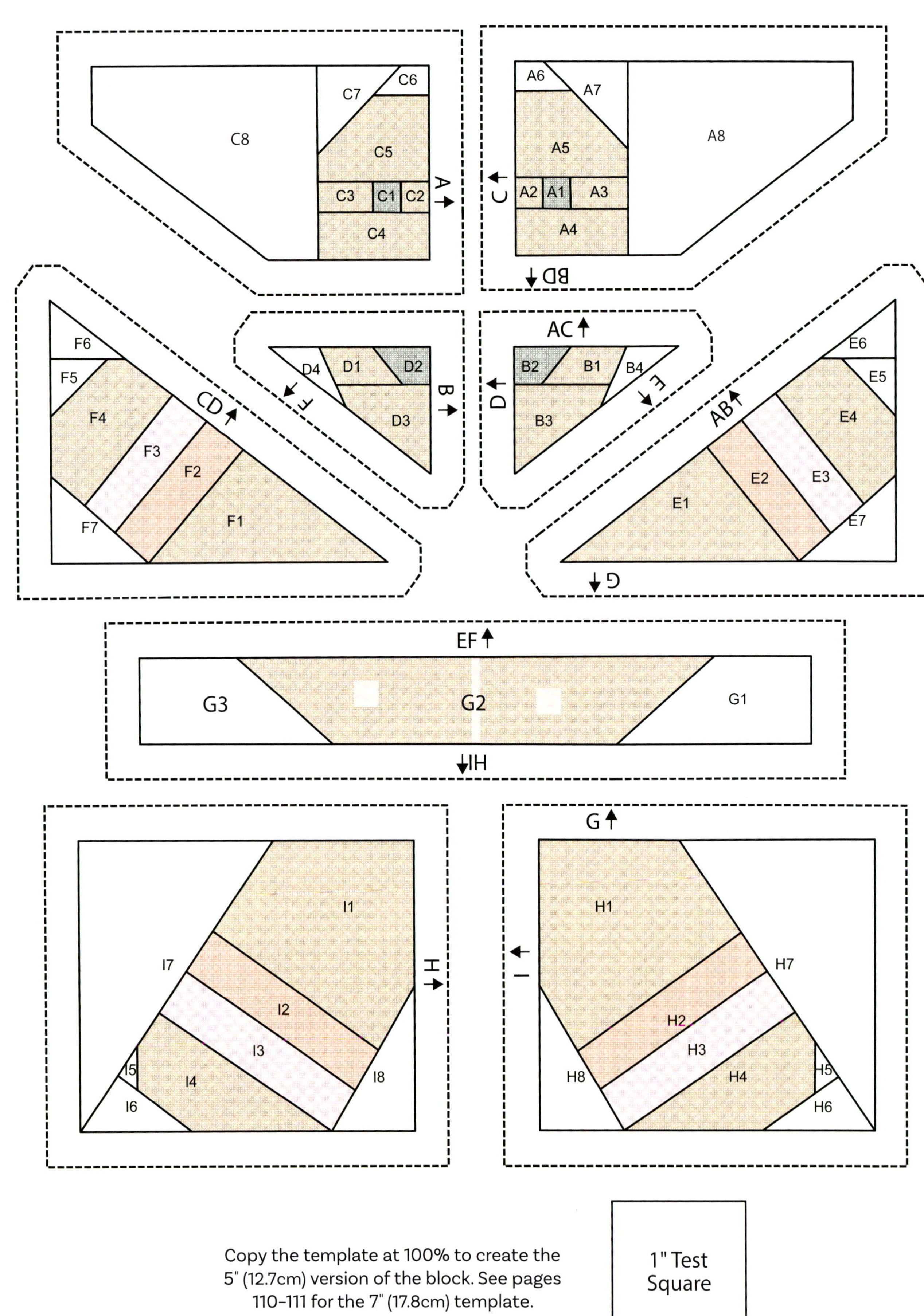

Copy the template at 100% to create the 5" (12.7cm) version of the block. See pages 110–111 for the 7" (17.8cm) template.

1" Test Square

Peppy Penguin

This guy is a sprinkle of holiday magic, all wrapped in feathers! I designed him to have a star on his belly, which not only symbolizes Christmas stars, but is also a nod to the timeless sawtooth star quilt block. It would be so cute to make a bunch of penguin friends and use them in a long lumbar pillow, or as festive coasters to make you smile every time you use them.

Assembly Instructions

1. Once you have all the sections pieced, attach section K to section I.
2. Attach unit IK to section B.
3. Attach unit BIK to section A.
4. Attach section F to section J.
5. Attach unit FJ to section D.
6. Attach unit DFJ to section G.
7. Attach unit DFGJ to section E.
8. Attach unit DEFGJ to section H.
9. Attach unit DEFGHJ to section C.
10. Attach unit CDEFGHJ to unit ABIK.
11. Attach unit ABCDEFGHIJK to section L.

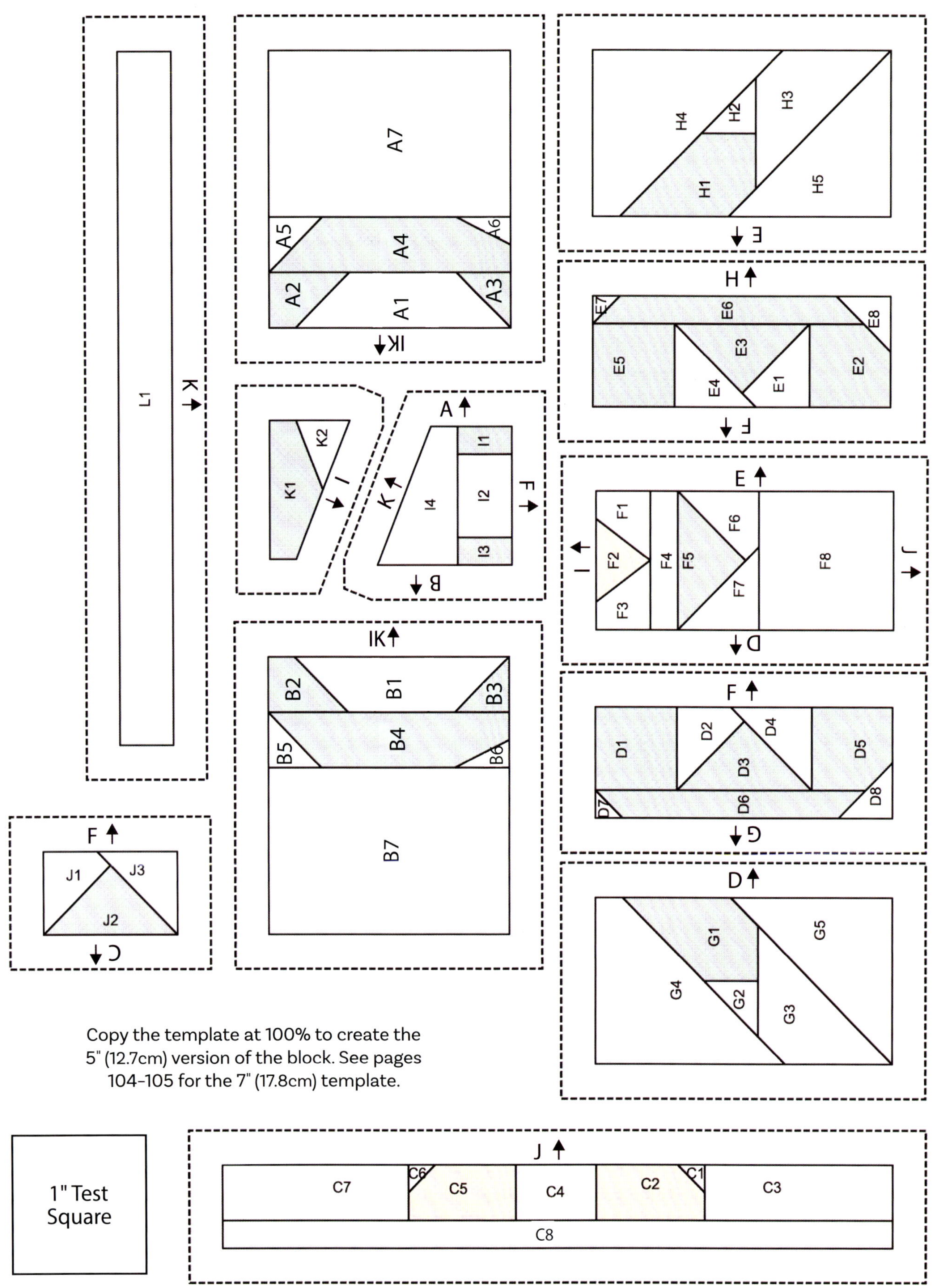

Copy the template at 100% to create the 5" (12.7cm) version of the block. See pages 104–105 for the 7" (17.8cm) template.

1" Test Square

Noble Nutcracker

Nutcrackers are one of the most collectible symbols of Christmas. First made by German woodcarvers in the 1600s, today the charming sentinels have become symbols of strength and protection.

Assembly Instructions

1. Once you have all the sections pieced, attach section A to section C.
2. Attach unit AC to section P.
3. Attach unit ACP to section O.
4. Attach unit ACOP to section J.
5. Attach unit ACJOP to section B.
6. Attach unit ABCJOP to section N.
7. Attach unit ABCJNOP to section M.
8. Attach unit ABCJMNOP to section H.
9. Attach section E to section I.
10. Attach unit EI to unit ABCHJMNOP.
11. Attach unit ABCEHIJMNOP to section G.
12. Attach section K to section D.
13. Attach section L to section F.
14. Attach unit DK to unit ABCEGHIJMNOP.
15. Attach unit LF to unit ABCDEGHIJKMNOP.

With such small pieces coming together to build the details, it can be tough to keep track of which fabrics make up which features. Here is a guide to keep track of your template and fabric pieces.

Background Pieces: B6, B8, D1, D3, D5, D6, E4, E5, F1, F3, F5, F6, G1, G5, H1, I4, J1, J3, M1, M3, N1, N3, O1, P1

Hair Pieces: A7, A8, C2, C7, O2, P2

Skin Pieces: A1, A3, A5, A6, A10, A11, C1, C6, H4, G4

Eye Pieces: A2, A4

Mouth Piece: C4

Mustache and Beard Pieces: A9, B1, C3, C5

Belt Piece: N2

Jacket Pieces: B2, B3, B4, B5, B7, M2

Pants Pieces: E3, I3

Boot Cuff Pieces: E2, I2

Boot Pieces: E1, I1

Shoulder Pieces: H2, G2

Sleeve Pieces: G3, H3

Hat Piece: J2

1 TBSP 15 ML
1 TSP 5 ML

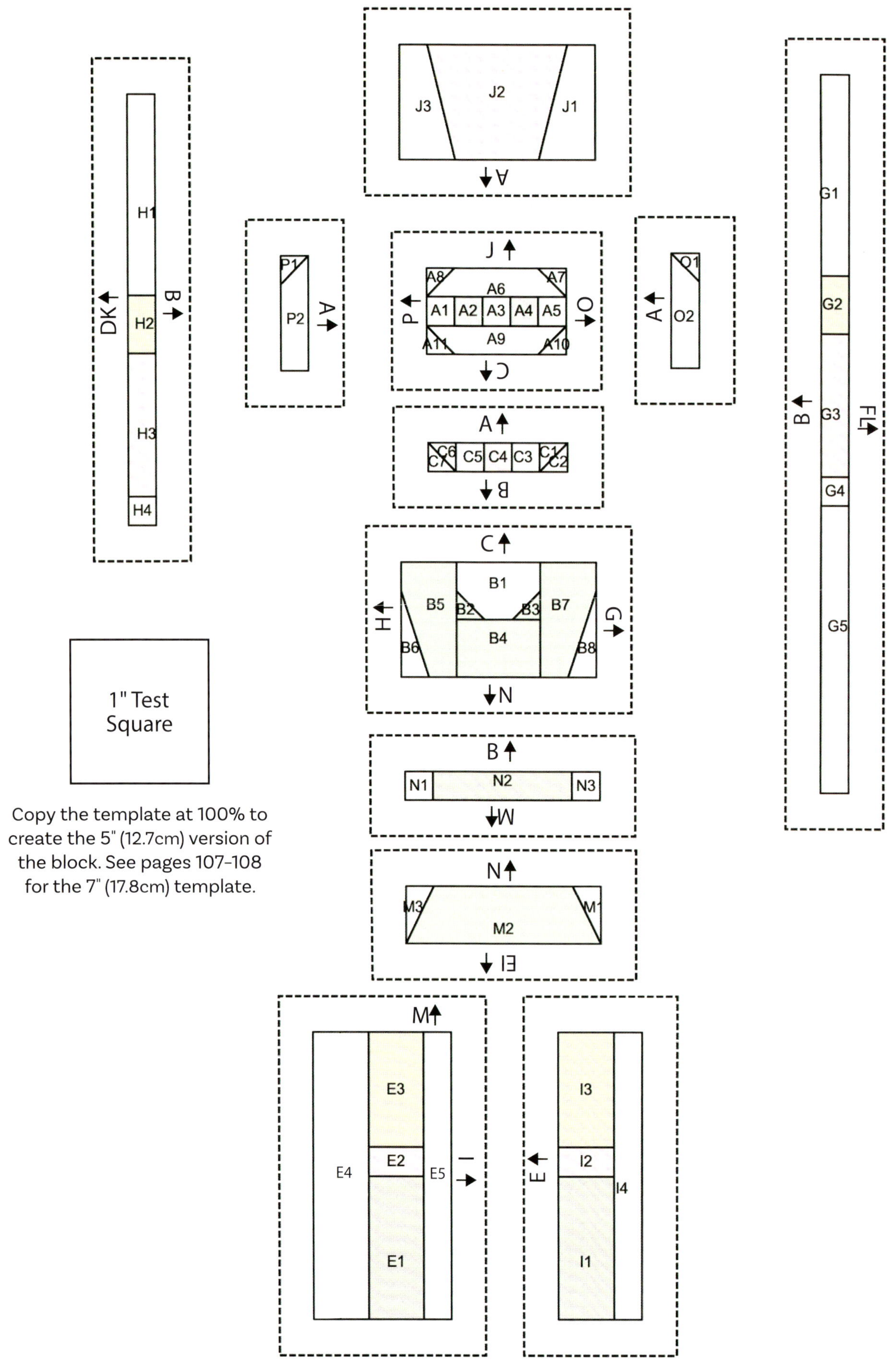

Copy the template at 100% to create the 5" (12.7cm) version of the block. See pages 107–108 for the 7" (17.8cm) template.

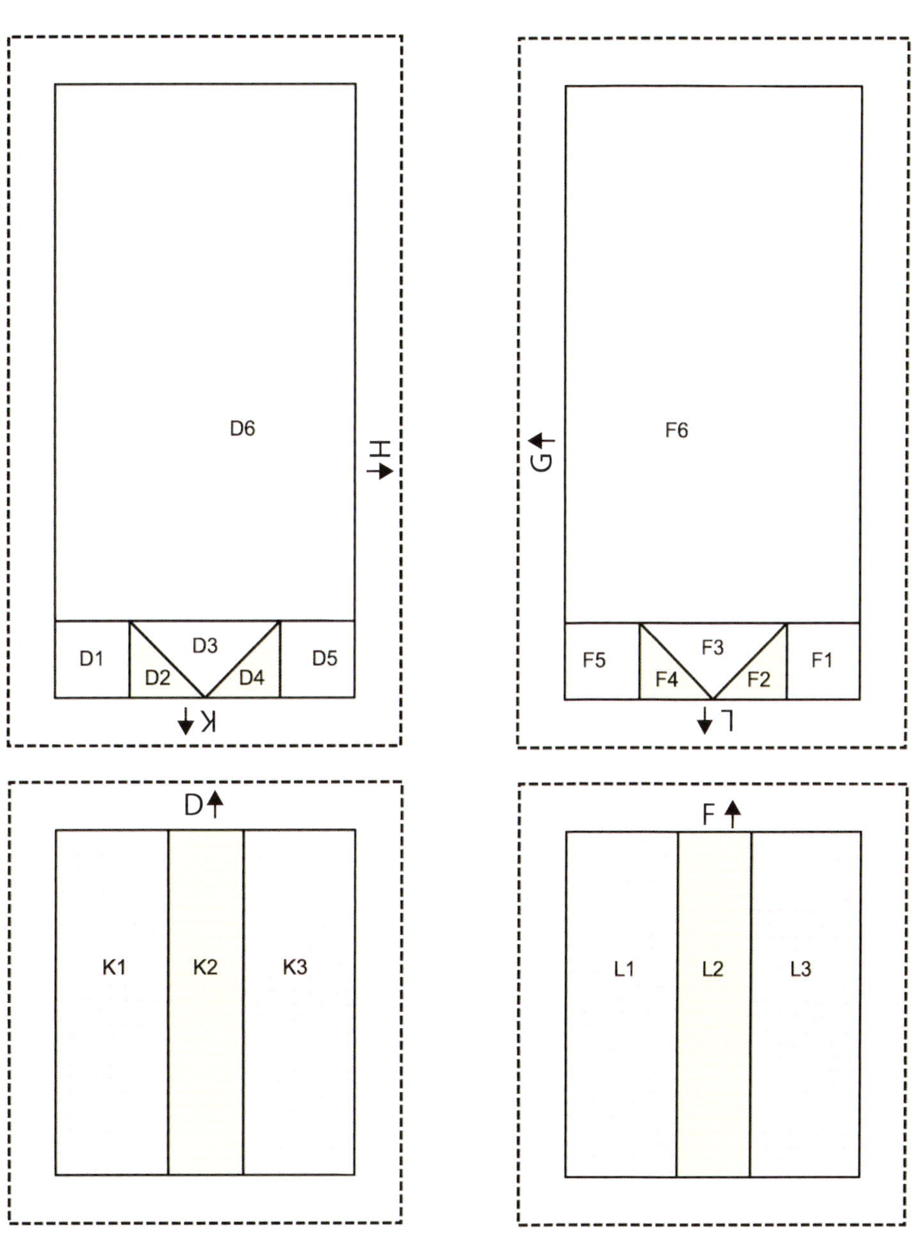

Copy the template at 100% to create the 5" (12.7cm) version of the block. See pages 107–108 for the 7" (17.8cm) template.

1" Test Square

Jolly Gnome

I might have a new love for gnomes after designing this block—isn't he just so cute! He is all about holiday magic, which is why he has a woodland Christmas tree hat. He will definitely bring a smile to your sewing room, and no doubt some extra sparkle to the project you use him in.

Assembly Instructions

1. Once you have all the sections pieced, attach section E to section A.
2. Attach unit AE to section D.
3. Attach unit ADE to section C.
4. Attach unit ACDE to section B.
5. Attach unit ABCDE to section H.
6. Attach unit ABCDEH to section G.
7. Attach unit ABCDEGH to section F.

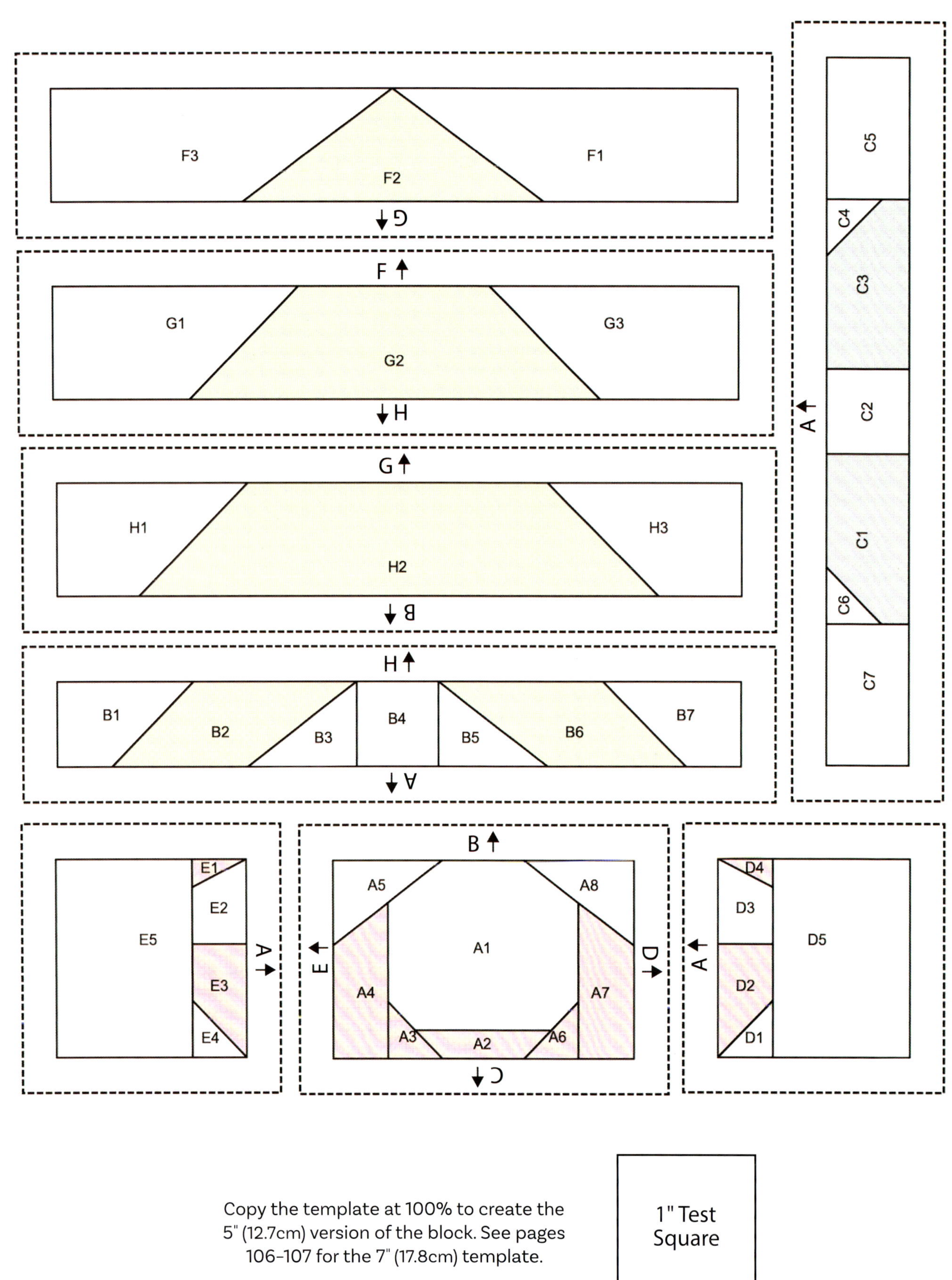

Copy the template at 100% to create the 5" (12.7cm) version of the block. See pages 106–107 for the 7" (17.8cm) template.

1" Test Square

A Parade of Projects

The block designs in this book work well on their own, whether framed or incorporated into other holiday decorations or accessories, but I've also included a few holiday projects to help inspire you! Follow the instructions to create larger projects like a gorgeous wall hanging, stockings, a garland, pillows, or table runners, or make smaller gifts, home items, and even reusable gift tags. Every project is customizable; combine the blocks as shown here or mix and match them all to highlight your favorites.

Ho Ho Ho Wall Hanging

Nothing says the holidays quite like a cheerful Ho Ho Ho greeting! This project is all about mixing and matching your favorite blocks to create something that feels uniquely yours. Go classic and cozy, bright and colorful, or anything in between. This design will fit right in with any holiday decor and make your space feel joyful, handmade, and full of personality.

Finished Size: 19" x 29" (48.3 x 73.7cm)

BLOCKS NEEDED*

- Three 7" (17.8cm) blocks
  - 1 x Candy Cane
  - 1 x Santa Hat
  - 1 x Christmas Tree

ADDITIONAL FABRIC

- ¼ yd. (22.9cm) or 1 fat quarter (45.7 x 55.9cm) letter fabric, cut as follows:
  - Twelve 2" x 7½" (5.1 x 19.1cm) rectangles
  - Three 2" x 2½" (5.1 x 6.4cm) rectangles
  - Six 2" (5.1cm) squares
- ½ yd. (45.7cm) background fabric, cut as follows:
  - Six 2½" x 3¼" (6.4 x 8.3cm) rectangles
  - Three 2" x 4½" (5.1 x 11.4cm) rectangles
  - Three 1¼" x 7½" (3.2 x 19.1cm) rectangles
  - Two 2" x 17¾" (5.1 x 45.1cm) rectangles
  - Two 1¼" x 17¾" (3.2 x 45.1cm) rectangles
- ⅝ yd. (57.2cm) backing fabric, cut as follows:
  - One 19" x 29" (48.3 x 73.7cm) rectangle
- ⅝ yd. (57.2cm) batting, cut as follows:
  - One 19" x 29" (48.3 x 73.7cm) rectangle
- ¼ yd. (22.9cm) binding fabric, cut as follows:
  - Three 2½" x WOF (6.4cm x WOF) strips

*The blocks listed here are the ones I used for the project. Feel free to mix and match any of the block designs in this book using the recommended template sizes to personalize your holiday project.

Make the Holiday FPP Blocks

1. Make the three holiday FPP blocks and set them aside.

Make the Letter H Units

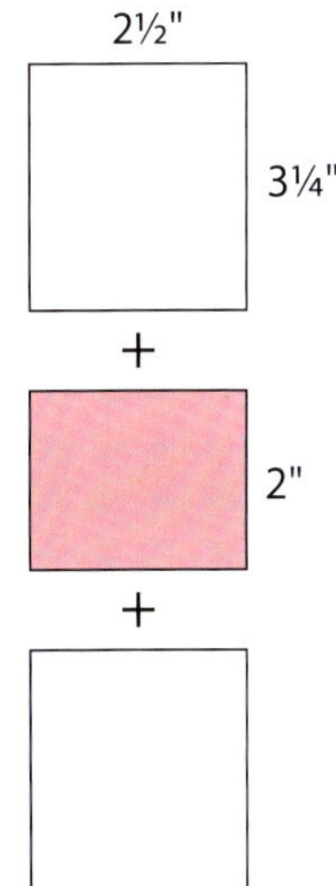

2. Assemble two 2½" x 3¼" (6.4 x 8.3cm) background fabric rectangles and one 2" x 2½" (5.1 x 6.4cm) letter fabric rectangle as shown.

3. Sew the pieces right sides together (RST). Press the seams toward the letter fabric. The finished unit will measure 2½" x 7½" (6.4 x 19.1cm).

TIP: A 1" (2.5cm) grid is a great option for quilting this project.

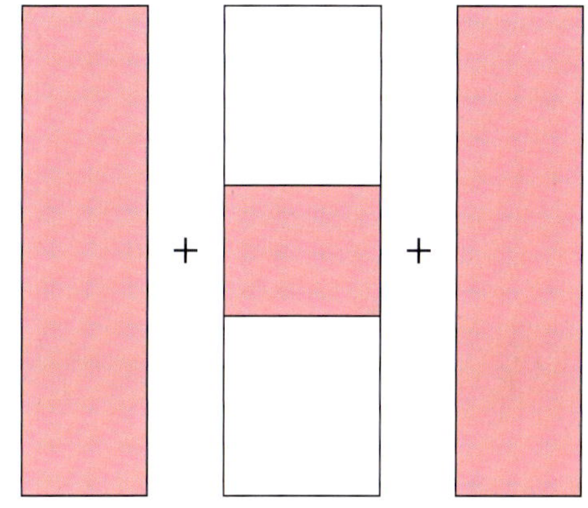

4. Place two 2" x 7½" (5.1 x 19.1cm) letter fabric rectangles on either side of the unit you just made.

5. Sew the pieces RST as shown. Press the seams toward the center unit. The finished unit will measure 5½" x 7½" (14 x 19.1cm).

6. Repeat steps 2–5 two more times. You will have a total of three letter H units.

Make the Letter O Units

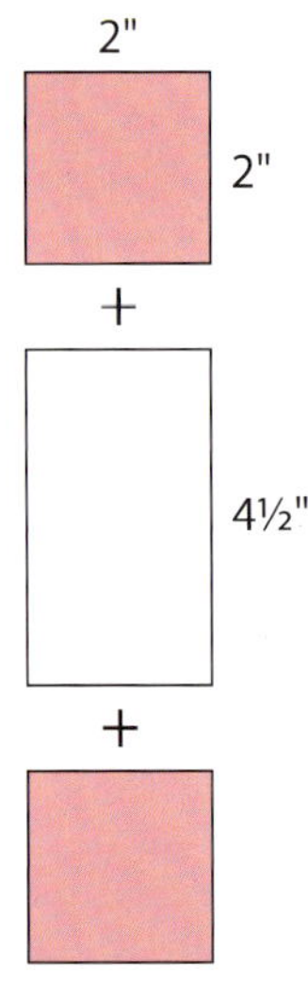

7. Assemble two 2" (5.1cm) letter fabric squares and one 2" x 4½" (5.1 x 11.4cm) background fabric rectangle as shown.

8. Sew the pieces RST as shown. Press the seams toward the letter fabric. The finished unit will measure 2" x 7½" (5.1 x 19.1cm).

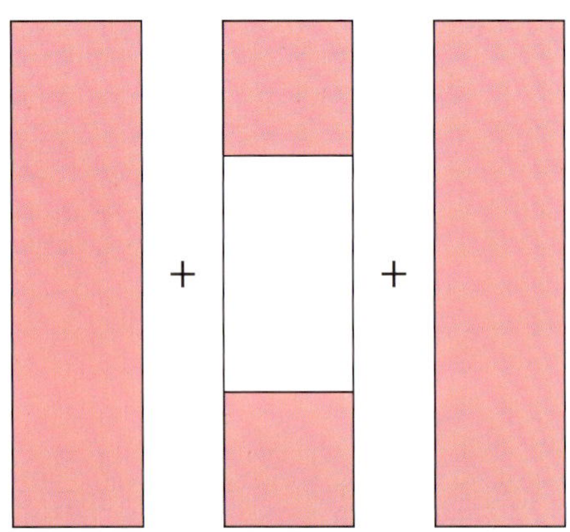

9. Place two 2" x 7½" (5.1 x 19.1cm) letter fabric rectangles on either side of the unit you just made.

10. Sew the pieces RST as shown. Press the seams toward the center unit. The finished unit will measure 5" x 7½" (12.7 x 19.1cm).

11. Repeat steps 7–10 two more times. You will have a total of three letter O units.

Assemble the HO Units

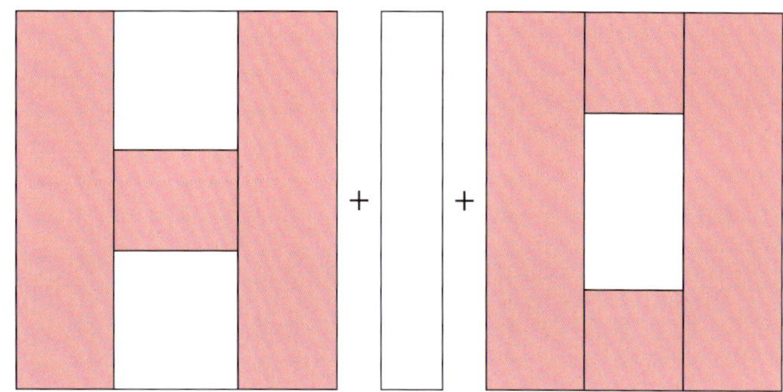

12. Assemble one letter H unit, one letter O unit, and one 1¼" x 7½" (3.2 x 19.1cm) background fabric rectangle as shown.

13. Sew the pieces RST as shown. Press the seams toward the letters. The finished unit will measure 10¾" x 7½" (27.3 x 19.1cm).

14. Repeat steps 12–13 two more times. You will have a total of three HO units.

Assemble and Finish the Wall Hanging

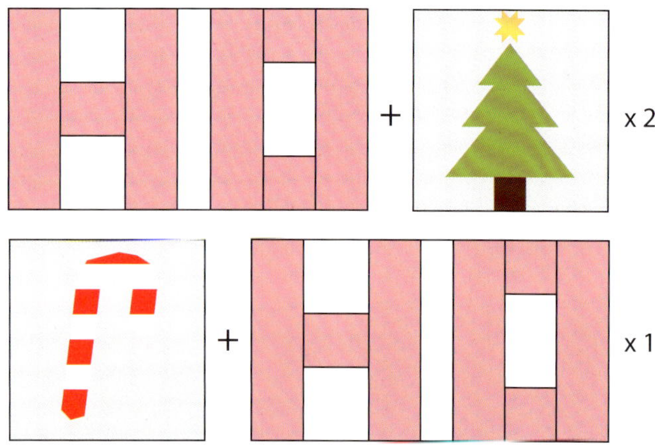

15. Assemble the three HO units and the three FPP units as shown to create two units with HO on the left and one unit with HO on the right.

16. Sew the pieces RST as shown. Press the seams toward the letters. The finished units will measure 17¾" x 7½" (45.1 x 19.1cm).

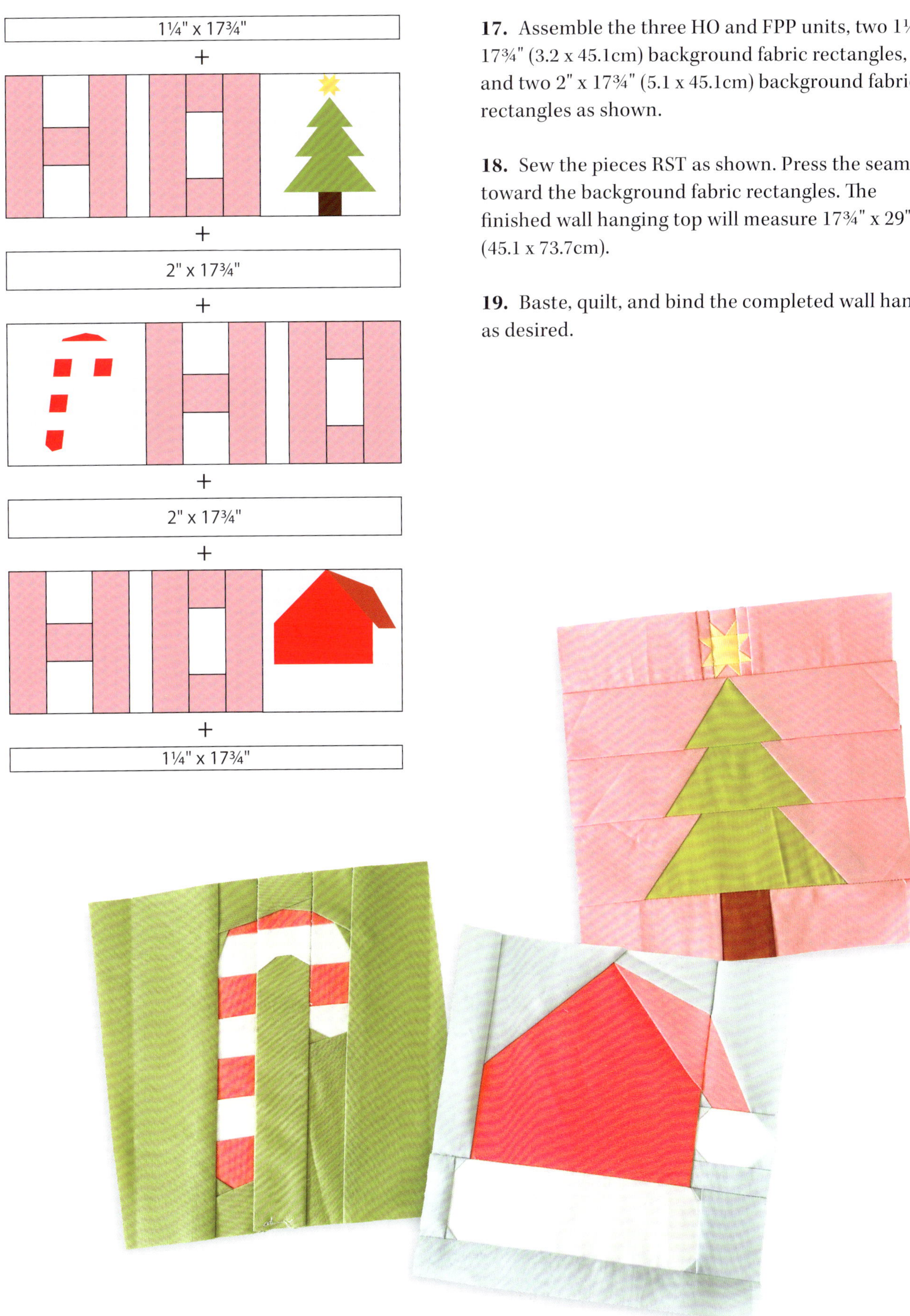

17. Assemble the three HO and FPP units, two 1¼" x 17¾" (3.2 x 45.1cm) background fabric rectangles, and two 2" x 17¾" (5.1 x 45.1cm) background fabric rectangles as shown.

18. Sew the pieces RST as shown. Press the seams toward the background fabric rectangles. The finished wall hanging top will measure 17¾" x 29" (45.1 x 73.7cm).

19. Baste, quilt, and bind the completed wall hanging as desired.

Cheerful Star Stocking

Hang up the holiday magic with this cheerful stocking! This project is the perfect place to mix prints, pile on color, let your favorite FPP blocks shine, and create a stocking that's just as joyful as what's tucked inside! You can make one for every family member or stitch up just a single statement piece. These stockings are made to be filled with treats, surprises, and lots of handmade love.

Finished Size: 12½" x 21" (31.8 x 53.3cm)

BLOCKS NEEDED*

- One 5" (12.7cm) block per stocking
  - 1 x Winter Star

ADDITIONAL FABRIC

- ½ yd. (45.7cm) main fabric, cut as follows:
  - Two 5½" x 2¾" (14 x 7cm) rectangles
  - One 3½" x 10" (9 x 25.4cm) rectangle
  - One 15½" (39.4cm) square
- ½ yd. (45.7cm) stocking back fabric, cut as follows:
  - One 25" x 15" (63.5 x 38.1cm) rectangle
- ¾ yd. (68.6cm) batting, cut as follows:
  - Two 16" x 24" (40.6 x 61cm) rectangles
- ¾ yd. (68.6cm) lining fabric, cut as follows:
  - With RS up, one stocking shape (see templates, pages 114–118) with toe pointing to the left
  - With RS down, one stocking shape (see templates, pages 114–118) with toe pointing to the left
- One 5" (12.7cm) length of any-width ribbon

*The blocks listed here are the ones I used for the project. Feel free to mix and match any of the block designs in this book using the recommended template sizes to personalize your holiday project.

Make the Lining

1. Place the front and back lining pieces RST with the toe facing to the left.

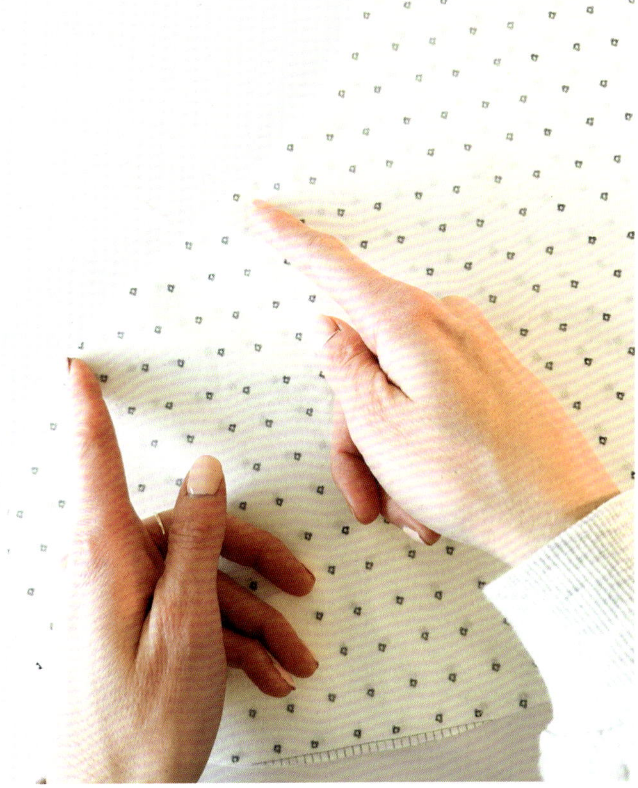

2. Sew the pieces together with a ¼" (6.4mm) seam allowance, leaving a 4" (10.2cm) gap along the upper edge of the toe piece where shown. *Note: Backstitch at the start and end of the gap.* Do not sew the top edge. Set the lining aside.

Make the Outer Stocking

3. Make the holiday FPP block.

4. Sew the two 5½" x 2¾" (14 x 7cm) main fabric rectangles RST on either side of the FPP block. Press the seams open.

5. Sew the 3½" x 10" (9 x 25.4cm) main fabric rectangle RST to the top of the FPP unit.

6. Lay down the 15½" (39.4cm) main fabric square RS up.

7. Line the FPP unit along the right side of the top edge of the main fabric square and flip it RST. Sew together and press.

8. Lay the batting piece down on a table and place the FPP stocking front unit RS up on top of it. Baste and quilt as desired.

TIP: Try quilting this project with a grid or straight lines that are ½" (1.3cm) apart.

9. Using the 25" x 15" (63.5 x 38.1cm) stocking back fabric rectangle, repeat step 8 to create the stocking back.

10. With the stocking front RS up, use the guides on the stocking templates (see pages 114–118) to line it up with your FPP unit. The toe should point to the left. Pin it in place and cut it out.

11. With the stocking back RS up, cut one stocking shape (see the templates, pages 114–118) with the toe pointing to the right.

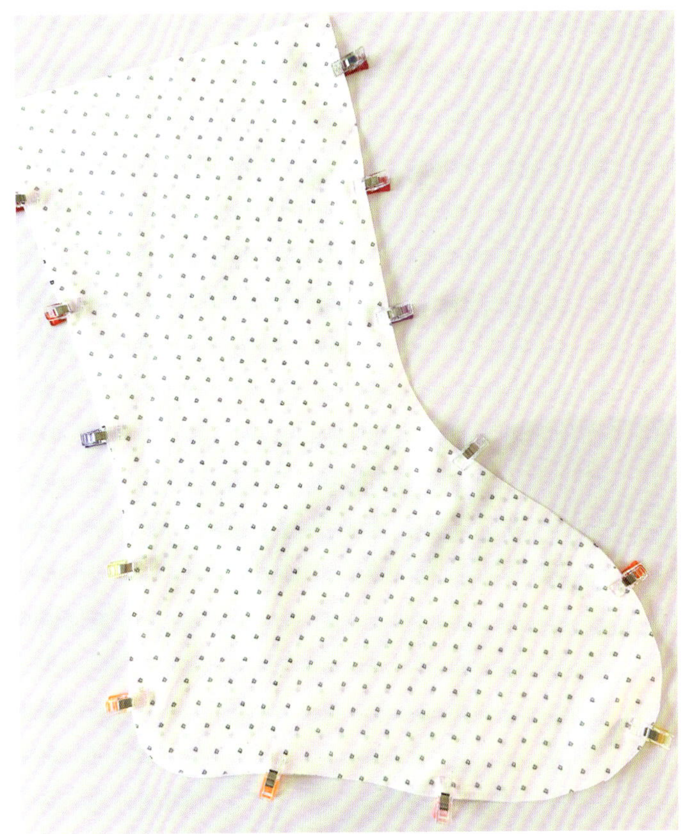

12. Lay the stocking front and stocking back RS together and clip or pin them in place. *Note: The example shown is using the lining fabric but the process is the same.* Sew the pieces together with a ¼" (6.4mm) seam allowance. Do not sew the top. Make sure to backstitch at the start and end of the opening.

13. Along curved edges, make small cuts in toward the stitching, taking care not to cut through the stitches. Turn this outer shell RS out and push out the curves. Give the unit a good press with the iron.

Assemble the Stocking

14. Place the outer shell inside the lining shell. They will be RST.

15. Place the ribbon loop in between the two layers RST with the stocking front. The ribbon loop will be pointing down with the raw edges lined up with the stocking edge. Pin it in place.

16. Making sure all the edges are aligned, pin together the lining and outer shell. Sew around the top opening of the stocking with ¼" (6.4mm) seam allowance, keeping the top edges even.

17. Pull the stocking RS out through the gap you left in the top edge of the toe of the lining.

18. Fold the gap in ¼" (6.4mm) and topstitch it closed. Push the lining down into the outer shell and topstitch around the perimeter. Your stocking is finished—enjoy!

Mini Banner Garland

Tiny banners, BIG cheer! This garland is the perfect way to showcase these fun blocks. Choose one theme for a polished look or combine animals, holly, and everything in between to create something more playful. Drape it across a mantel or over a shelf or doorway, or around your sewing space to let your favorite fabrics do the celebrating.

Finished Size: 5" x 46" (12.7cm x 1.2m)

BLOCKS NEEDED*

- Six 5" (12.7cm) blocks
  - 1 x Holly Berries
  - 1 x Christmas Tree
  - 1 x Cozy Mittens
  - 1 x Candy Cane
  - 1 x Santa Hat
  - 1 x Jolly Gnome

ADDITIONAL FABRIC

- Six 5½" (14cm) fusible fleece squares
- Six 5½" (14cm) backing fabric squares
- One 18" (45.7cm) square bias tape fabric

*The blocks listed here are the ones I used for the project. Feel free to mix and match any of the block designs in this book using the recommended template sizes to personalize your holiday project.

Make the Banner Blocks

1. Make the holiday FPP blocks.

2. Fuse the fusible fleece to the back of the FPP blocks following the manufacturer's instructions.

3. Lay the FPP block RS up, then lay the backing fabric RS down on top of that. Pin it in place.

4. Sew around the perimeter of the square with a ¼" (6.4mm) seam allowance, leaving a 3" (7.6cm) gap along one of the sides.

5. Trim the corners to reduce bulk.

6. Turn the block RS out and press it, taking care to press in ¼" (6.4mm) of the gap opening.

7. Clip or pin the gap closed.

8. Topstitch the gap closed, then continue topstitching around the perimeter of the block.

9. Repeat steps 2–8 for all remaining FPP blocks.

Make the Bias Tape

10. Cut the 18" (45.7cm) bias tape fabric square in half diagonally.

11. Match two short edges RS together as shown and sew along the edge with a ¼" (6.4mm) seam allowance. Press the seam open.

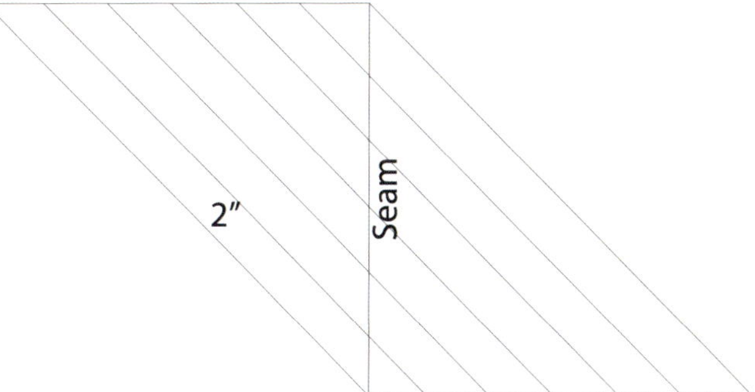

12. Cut 2" (5.1cm) strips from the unit you made in step 11 as shown. Sew the strips together along the short edges.

13. Fold the bias tape in half lengthwise, WS together, and press. Open it back up, then fold the long edges in to meet the center crease and press. Fold the strip in half again and press.

14. Open the bias tape up and position your blocks inside it, lining up the edges. Space the blocks along the tape as desired. Fold the bias tape and pin it in place.

15. Starting at the beginning of the bias tape, topstitch it closed to secure the blocks. Keep the bias tape ends as long or as short as you need to easily hang your banner as desired.

Merry Pillow Covers

Pick your block, pick your fabrics, and let's make a pillow! This cover lets your favorite FPP block take center stage while you play with fabrics that match your festive style. Feeling extra fancy? Add the optional ruffle for a sweet and playful frame or keep it simple for a clean and classic look. However you make it, this pillow is all about color, texture, and cozy seasonal charm.

Finished Size: 19" (48.3cm) square without ruffle, 22" (55.9cm) square with ruffle

BLOCKS NEEDED*

- One 7" (17.8cm) block
  - 1 x Holly Berries or Happy Snowman

ADDITIONAL FABRIC

- ½ yd. (45.7cm) pillow front fabric, cut as follows:
  - Two 6¾" x 7½" (17.2 x 19.1cm) rectangles
  - Two 20" x 6¾" (50.8 x 17.2cm) rectangles
- ⅔ yd. (61cm) backing fabric, cut as follows:
  - Two 20" x 14" (50.8 x 35.6cm) rectangles
- ¾ yd. (68.6cm) batting, cut as follows:
  - Two 16" x 24" (40.6 x 61cm) rectangles
- One 21" (53.3cm) square of batting
- A 20" (50.8cm) square pillow form
- Three 4" (10.2cm) x WOF ruffle strips, optional

*The blocks listed here are the ones I used for the project. Feel free to mix and match any of the block designs in this book using the recommended template sizes to personalize your holiday project.

Make the Pillow Front

1. Make the holiday FPP block.

2. Sew the two 6¾" x 7½" (17.2 x 19.1cm) pillow front fabric rectangles RST on either side of the FPP block. Press the seams toward the pillow front fabric.

3. Sew the two 20" x 6¾" (50.8 x 17.2cm) pillow front fabric rectangles RST to the top and bottom of the unit you made in step 2. Press the seams toward the top and bottom pillow front fabric rectangles.

4. Lay your pillow front piece RS up on top of the batting square. Quilt as desired.

Prepare the Backing Rectangles

5. Take one backing fabric rectangle and place it RS down. Fold the long top edge down ¼" (6.4mm) and press it. Fold it down another ¼" (6.4mm) and press it again. Topstitch along the folded edge to create a hem. *Note: If you are using directional fabric, make sure the print is oriented the way you want it.*

6. Repeat step 5 with the remaining backing fabric rectangle. If you're adding a ruffle, continue to the next step. If you're not adding a ruffle proceed to step 17 under the Assemble the Pillow header on page 77.

Add the Ruffle

7. Sew each ruffle strip RST along the short edges. Press.

8. Fold the long strip WST along the long side and press.

9. Set your stitch length as long as it will go. Sew a basting stitch ¼" (0.6cm) in from the edge, making sure to leave long tails (about 4" [10.2cm] long) at the start and end.

10. Sew another basting stitch ¼" (0.6cm) in from the one you just sewed, making sure to leave long tails at the start and end.

11. Pick which side of the ruffle will be the "wrong" side. Tie knots at the start and end of each basting stitch row with the two long tails you left.

12. Slowly pull the two ends on the "right" side of the ruffle. Slide the bunched "ruffle" to the middle of the strip. Continue pulling and sliding the ruffle until you reach your desired amount of "ruffle-ness" on this side. Repeat on the other side of the ruffle.

13. When your ruffle is as ruffled as you would like, give it a press across the entire piece.

14. Starting on the long edge of the pillow front piece, pin the ruffle around the entire perimeter. Leave a tail at the start and end of at least 10" (25.4cm).

15. Sew around the perimeter with an ⅛" (3.2mm) seam allowance. As you get closer to the starting point, leave a 6" (15.2cm) gap and backstitch.

16. Sew the two ruffle ends together with a French seam: On the wrong side of your ruffle, mark a line where the two fabrics will intersect on each piece. Sew the fabric WST with a ⅜" (9.5mm) seam allowance, then trim the seam allowance and press it open. Fold the fabric RST to encase the raw edges, then press and stitch again with a slightly wider ¼" (6.4mm) seam allowance, enclosing the first seam completely for a neat finish.

Assemble the Pillow

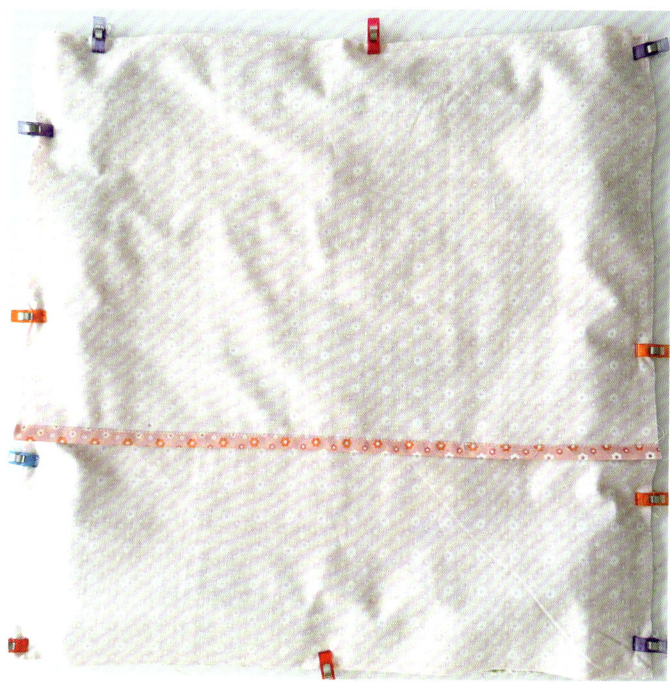

17. Layer the backing pieces RS down on top of the RS-up pillow front, with the hemmed edges overlapping in the center. Take care that the prints are correctly oriented and pin or clip it in place.

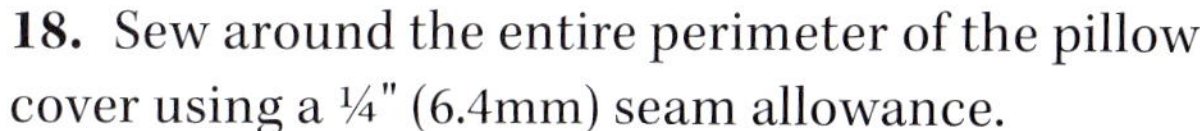

18. Sew around the entire perimeter of the pillow cover using a ¼" (6.4mm) seam allowance.

19. Trim the corners and turn the pillow cover RS out through the backing pieces.

20. Insert your pillow form and enjoy!

Festive Hot Pad

Bring a little handmade magic into the heart of your home with this hot pad! Featuring your favorite FPP block, this cheerful dining room essential adds a lovely touch to a cozy Christmas kitchen and serves a practical purpose in festive holiday spreads!

Finished Size: 15½" x 17½" (39.4 x 44.5cm)

BLOCKS NEEDED*

- One 7" (17.8cm) block
  - 1 x Hot Cocoa Mug

ADDITIONAL FABRIC

- 1 fat quarter (45.7 x 55.9cm) main fabric, cut as follows:
  - Two 5" x 7½" (12.7 x 19.1cm) rectangles
  - Two 3" x 16½" (7.6 x 41.9cm) rectangles
  - One 2¼" x 6" (5.7 x 15.2cm) rectangle
- 1 fat quarter (45.7 x 55.9cm) backing fabric, cut as follows:
  - One 12½ x 16½" (31.8 x 41.9cm) rectangles
- One 12½" x 16½" (31.8 x 41.9cm) rectangle heat-resistant insulated batting
- ¼ yd. (22.9cm) binding fabric, cut as follows:
  - Two 2½" x WOF (6.4cm x WOF) strips

*The blocks listed here are the ones I used for the project. Feel free to mix and match any of the block designs in this book using the recommended template sizes to personalize your holiday project.

Make the Holiday FPP Blocks

1. Make the holiday FPP block.

Assemble the Hot Pad

2. Sew one of the 5" x 7½" (12.7 x 19.1cm) main fabric rectangles RST to the left edge of the FPP block. Press.

3. Repeat step 2 on the right edge of the block. Press.

4. Sew one of the 3" x 16½" (7.6 x 41.9cm) main fabric rectangles RST to the top of the FPP unit. Press.

5. Repeat step 4 on the bottom of the FPP unit. Press.

6. Lay the backing piece RS down, then layer on the batting and the FPP unit RS up to make a quilt sandwich. Baste and quilt as desired.

Add the Hanging Loop and Binding

7. Fold the remaining main fabric rectangle in half lengthwise, WST, and press it. Open it back up, then fold the long edges in to meet the center crease and press. Fold the strip in half again and press. Topstitch along both long edges.

8. Sew the two binding strips RST along the short edges and press the seam open. Fold the binding strip in half lengthwise, WST, and press it.

TIP: Try quilting your hot pad with a straight-line grid or free-motion swirls, or simply outline your block.

9. Lay your quilted unit RS down and pin the hanging loop RS up where you want to place it, aligning the raw edges. Sew it in place with an ⅛" (3.2mm) seam allowance. Place the binding and sew around the perimeter to attach it to the back side of the hot pad, joining the ends.

10. Fold the binding around to the front and stitch it down on the front side of the hot pad.

11. Fold the hanging tab up against the binding and topstitch it in place.

Warm and Toasty Coasters

These merry little mug rugs are the perfect small-but-mighty holiday make! Choose your favorite FPP block (or make a whole variety), pair it with your favorite fabrics, and stitch up a cozy resting spot for your cocoa, coffee, or a plate of warm Christmas cookies. They're quick, fun, and make the sweetest handmade gifts—if you can bear to part with them!

Finished Size: 5" (12.7cm) square

BLOCKS NEEDED*

- One 5" (12.7cm) block per coaster
  - 1 x Peppy Penguin, Candy Cane, or Hot Cocoa Mug

ADDITIONAL FABRIC

- One 6½" (16.5cm) square batting
- One 5½" (14cm) square backing fabric
- Ribbon trim, optional

Make the Holiday FPP Block

1. Make one holiday FPP block.

2. Lay the holiday FPP block RS up on top of the batting square, then quilt as desired.

3. Square up the quilted block and trim off any excess batting. If you're adding ribbon trim, continue to the next step. If you're not adding ribbon trim, proceed to step 6 under the Finish the Coaster header.

Add the Ribbon Trim

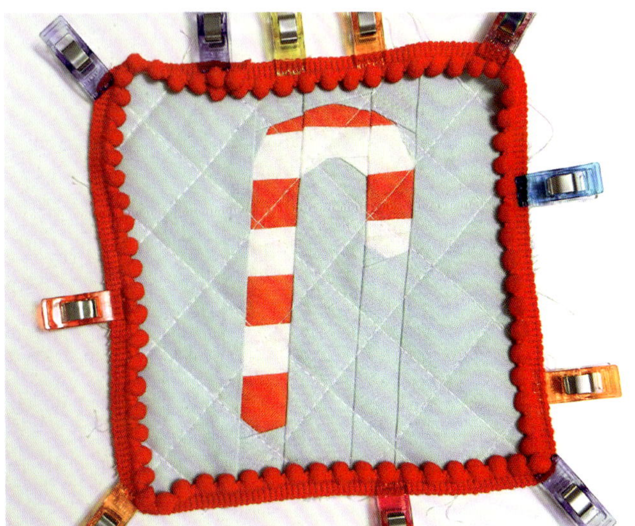

4. After quilting the unit, clip or pin the ribbon around the perimeter RST, matching up the raw edges.

5. Sew the ribbon in place with a ¼" (6.4mm) seam allowance.

Finish the Coaster

6. Place the quilted unit RST on top of the backing fabric square and pin it in place.

7. Sew around the perimeter with ¼" (6.4mm) seam allowance, leaving a 3" (7.6cm) gap along one of the edges. Make sure to backstitch at the beginning and end of the gap.

8. Trim the corners to reduce bulk.

9. Turn the coaster RS out through the opening you left, then use a point turner or sharp pair of scissors to push out the corners, taking care not to poke through any stitches.

10. Press the coaster flat with an iron, making sure to fold in the gap opening ¼" (6.4mm) to enclose the raw edge.

11. Topstitch around the perimeter of the coaster and you're done!

Delightful Zipper Pouch

If you love giving handmade gifts, this project is for you! These zipper pouches let your favorite FPP blocks take center stage while you create something both beautiful and practical. Make one for everyone on your list and fill them with their favorite things! Stuffed with chocolates, collectibles, or sewing goodies, these are presents that feel extra thoughtful and personal.

Finished Size: 5" (12.7cm) square or 7" (17.8cm) square

BLOCKS NEEDED*

- One 5" (12.7cm) block or one 7" (17.8cm) block
  - 1 x Hot Cocoa Mug

ADDITIONAL FABRIC

- One fat eighth (22.9 x 55.9cm) main pouch back fabric, cut as follows:
  - One 5½" (12.7cm) square or one 7½" (17.8cm) square
- One fat eighth (22.9 x 55.9cm) accent fabric, cut as follows:
  - Two 5½" (12.7cm) squares or two 7½" (17.8cm) squares, for lining
  - Two 1½" (3.8cm) squares or two 2½" (6.4cm) squares, for zipper tabs
- Two 5½" (12.7cm) squares or two 7½" (17.8cm) squares fusible fleece
- One 4½" (11.4cm) or one 6½" (16.5cm) zipper

*The blocks listed here are the ones I used for the project. Feel free to mix and match any of the block designs in this book using the recommended template sizes to personalize your holiday project.

Make the Holiday FPP Block

1. Make one holiday FPP block in your chosen size. Set it aside.

Add the Zipper Tabs

2. Lay one zipper tab fabric square RS down. Fold one long edge in ¼" (6.4mm) and press it. Repeat with the opposite edge. Once both sides are pressed, fold the tab in half and press it again. Repeat with the other zipper tab fabric square.

3. Slide one zipper end into one of the folded zipper tab fabric pieces to create a sandwich. Clip it in place and repeat on the other end of the zipper.

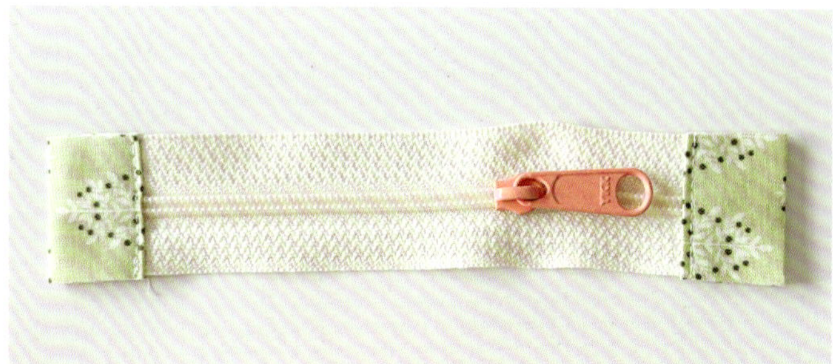

4. Straight stitch along the inner edge of each zipper tab. Trim the sides of the zipper tabs to line up with the zipper tape.

Assemble the Pouch

5. Fuse one fusible fleece square to your FPP block and one to the pouch back fabric following the manufacturer's instructions.

6. Lay the FPP block RS up and place the zipper on top of that RS down. Center the zipper on the block—there should be about ½" (1.3cm) on each side.

7. Lay one lining piece RS down on top of the zipper, creating a sandwich with the zipper in the middle. Clip it in place.

8. Switch to a zipper foot and sew ¼" (6.4mm) in along the top. Press both fabrics away from the zipper. *Optional: Topstitch along the sewn edge.*

9. Lay the pouch back fabric RS up, then lay the zipper unit on top RS down, lining up the zipper with the top edge of the pouch back fabric.

10. Lay the other lining piece on top of the zipper RS down, aligning the top edge with the edge of the zipper. Clip it in place.

11. Sew along the edge just as you did in step 8. Press both fabric pieces away from the zipper. *Optional: Topstitch along the sewn edge.*

12. Unzip the zipper about three-quarters open.

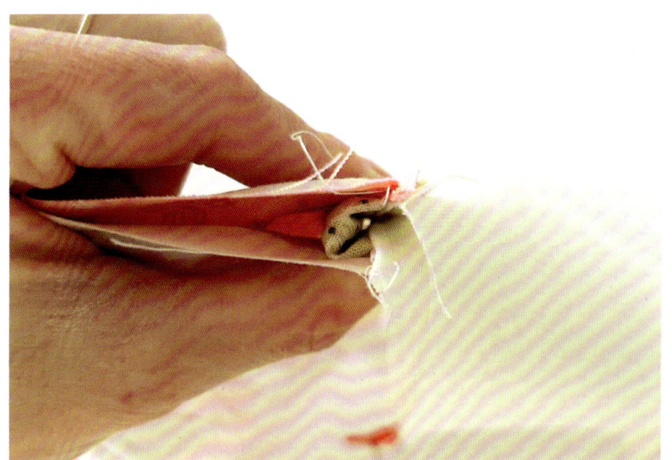

13. Line up the front and back pieces RST and pin them in place. Do the same for the lining pieces. Fold the zipper tabs inward toward the front and back pouch pieces.

14. Using a ¼" (6.4mm) seam allowance, sew around the entire perimeter of the pouch, leaving a 4" (10.2cm) gap open on the bottom edge of the lining. Trim each corner as shown, taking care to not cut any stitches.

15. Turn the pouch RS out through the open gap. Use a point turner or scissors to push out and make each corner nice and sharp.

16. Fold the raw edges of the lining gap in ¼" (6.4mm) and pin them together. Sew along the edge to close up the gap.

17. Fold the lining into the pouch and you are done! Fill your finished pouch with plenty of holiday treats!

Perfect Oven Mitts

These oven mitts combine your favorite blocks and complementary fabrics to add joy to your holiday kitchen decor. Stitch up a set to use while baking all your holiday treats or wrap them up for the favorite cook in your life. These are the kind of gift that's both beautiful and wonderfully useful.

Finished Size: 7½" x 34" (19.1 x 86.4cm)

BLOCKS NEEDED*

- Two 5" (12.7cm) blocks with borders (see the box below) or two 7" (17.8cm) blocks
  - 2 x Christmas Tree or Red-Nosed Reindeer

ADDITIONAL FABRIC

- One 7½" x WOF (19.1cm x WOF) main fabric strip, cut as follows:
  - One 7½" x 34" (19.1cm x 86.4cm) rectangle
- ½ yd. (45.7cm) backing fabric, cut as follows:
  - Two 7½" (31.8cm) squares
  - One 7½" x 34" (19.1cm x 86.4cm) rectangle
- ½ yd. (45.7cm) heat-resistant insulated batting, cut as follows:
  - Two 7½" (31.8cm) squares
  - One 7½" x 34" (19.1cm x 86.4cm) rectangle
- 1 fat quarter (45.7 x 55.9cm) binding fabric, cut as follows:
  - Two 2" x 7½" (5.1 x 31.8cm) rectangles
  - One 18" (45.7cm) square, for bias binding

*The blocks listed here are the ones I used for the project. Feel free to mix and match any of the block designs in this book using the recommended template sizes to personalize your holiday project.

Make the Holiday FPP Blocks

1. Make the two holiday FPP blocks.

Make the Oven Mitt Pieces

2. Create three layered sections: Two for the end pockets and one longer main piece. Start by laying out all three pieces of backing fabric RS down. Layer the batting pieces on top of that, then top with the holiday FPP blocks and the main fabric rectangle RS up.

3. Baste and quilt each section as desired.

Which Size Blocks to Start With

In this project, you'll be rounding the corners of your holiday FPP blocks. You can start with two 7" (17.8cm) blocks, which will have enough negative space to allow for the rounded corners, or you can start with two 5" (12.7cm) blocks and add a border, which is what I did for my example pieces.

To add a border, sew two 1½" x 5½" (3.8 x 14cm) fabric rectangles RST to the left and right edges of your FPP block, then press. Sew two 1½" x 7½" (3.8 x 19.1cm) fabric rectangles RST to the top and bottom edges of your FPP block, then press.

Add Binding to the Pocket Units

4. Fold one 2" x 7½" (5.1 x 31.8cm) binding fabric rectangle in half lengthwise WST. Clip or pin this folded piece on top of the backing side of one of the pocket units, matching the raw edges together. Sew it in place with a ¼" (6.4mm) seam allowance.

5. Fold the binding over to the main side of the pocket unit and sew ⅛" (3.2mm) in from the folded edge.

6. Repeat with the second pocket unit.

Assemble the Oven Mitt Pieces

7. Place the main section RS up and align the pocket units RS up on top of either end as shown. Pin them in place.

8. Stitch them in place with a ⅛" (3.2mm) seam allowance along the three outer edges of the pockets. Do not stitch along the pocket binding edges.

Finish the Oven Mitt

9. Using the template on page 113, round the outer corners of each pocket. Restitch the corners with a ⅛" (3.2mm) seam allowance.

10. Make bias binding with the 18" (45.7cm) binding fabric square (see page 72).

11. Bind the oven mitt, starting on the backing side and lining up the raw edges of the bias binding and the oven mitt. Sew around the perimeter with a ¼" (6.4mm) seam allowance. Join the binding edges using your preferred method.

12. Flip the oven mitt over and stitch the binding down on the front ⅛" (3.2mm) in from the folded edge. Your oven mitt is finished—use and enjoy!

Reusable Fabric Gift Tags

Tiny, fun, and endlessly reusable, these gift tags add a perfect handmade pop to every present! Stitch them up once and enjoy them year after year.

Finished Size: 3" (7.6cm) square

BLOCKS NEEDED*

- One 3" (7.6cm) block, see Resizing the Patterns on page 17
  - 1 x Christmas Tree or Santa Hat

ADDITIONAL FABRIC

- One 4½" (11.4cm) felt backing square
- One 3½" x 2½" (8.9 x 6.4cm) felt pocket rectangle
- One ½" x 4" (1.3 x 10.2cm) ribbon
- Hot glue gun and glue

*The blocks listed here are the ones I used for the project. Feel free to mix and match any of the block designs in this book using the recommended template sizes to personalize your holiday project.

Make the Holiday FPP Block

1. Make the resized holiday FPP block.

Assemble the Tag Front

2. Lay the holiday FPP block RS up on top of the felt backing piece. Pin them together.

3. Sew around the outside edge of the FPP block with a tight zigzag stitch.

4. Use pinking shears to cut around the entire perimeter of the FPP block, about ⅛" (3.2mm) away from the zigzag stitch.

Add the Ribbon and Pocket

5. Fold the ribbon in half and use the hot glue to glue it onto the back of the tag.

6. Sew the remaining felt piece onto the back of the tag, lining up the bottom edges. Use a straight stitch about an ⅛" (3.2mm) in from the edge.

7. Write a nice note to someone you love, place it in the pocket, and you're ready to gift!

Additional Block Templates

Copy the following templates at 100% to create the 7" (17.8cm) versions of the blocks. You can also download all the pattern files at *foxpatterns.com/wonderful-world-christmas-blocks*.

Scan the QR code to quickly access the digital template page.

1" Test Square

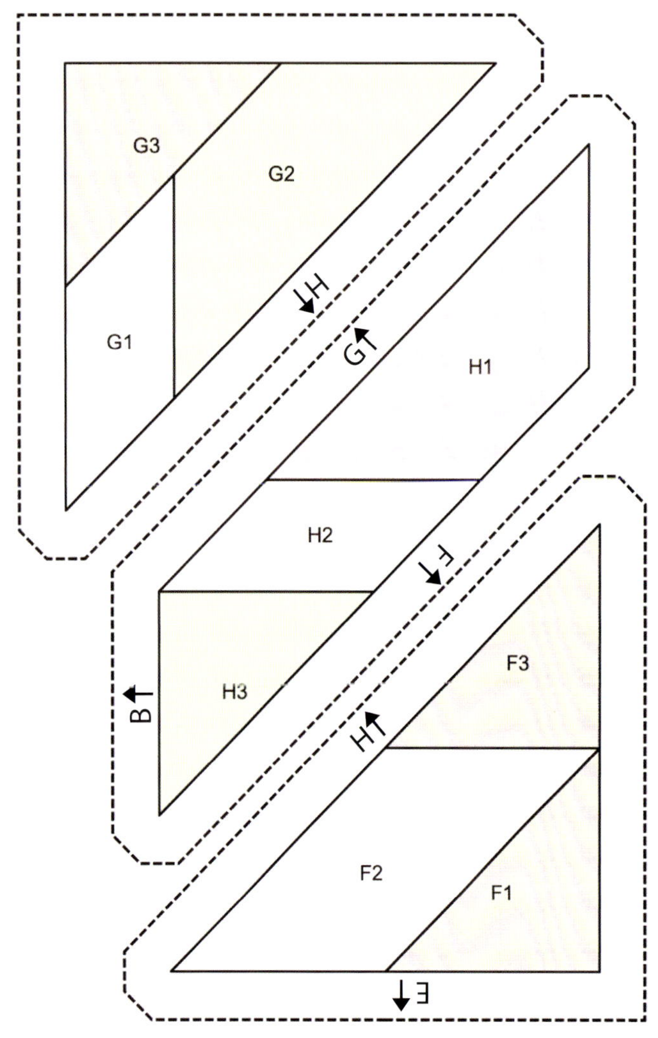

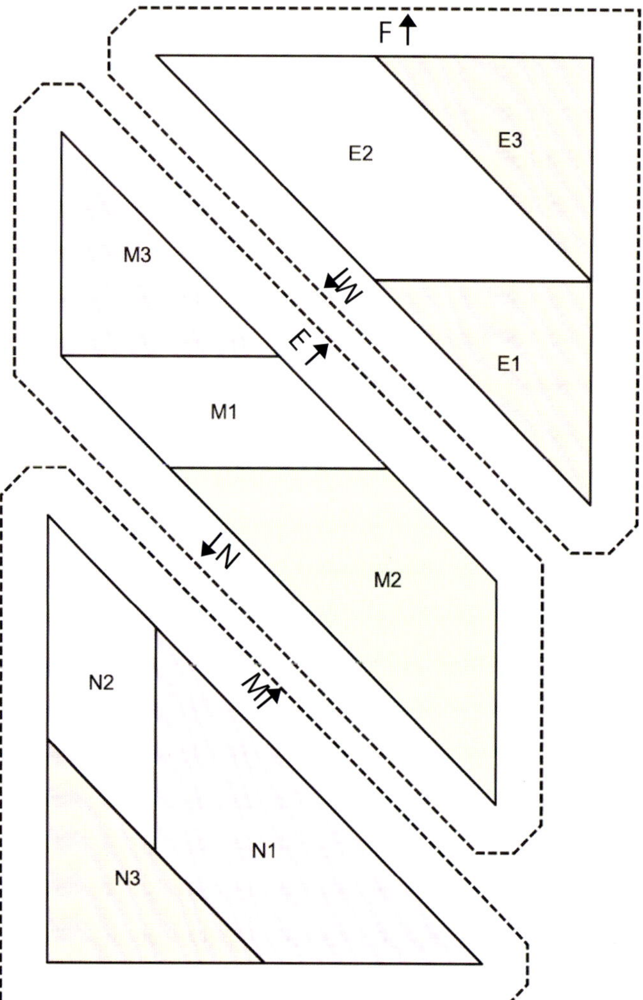

Winter Star, page 20

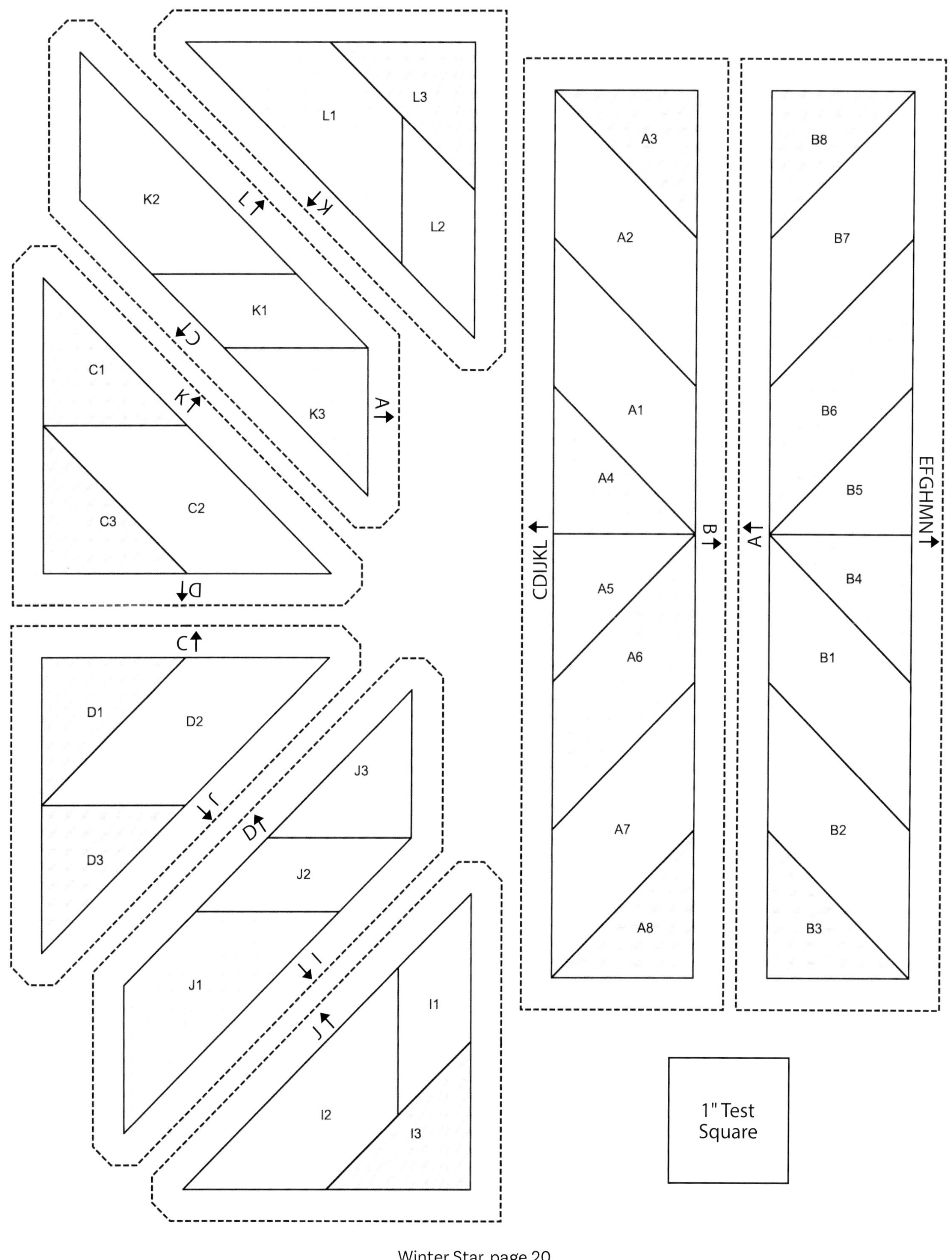

Winter Star, page 20

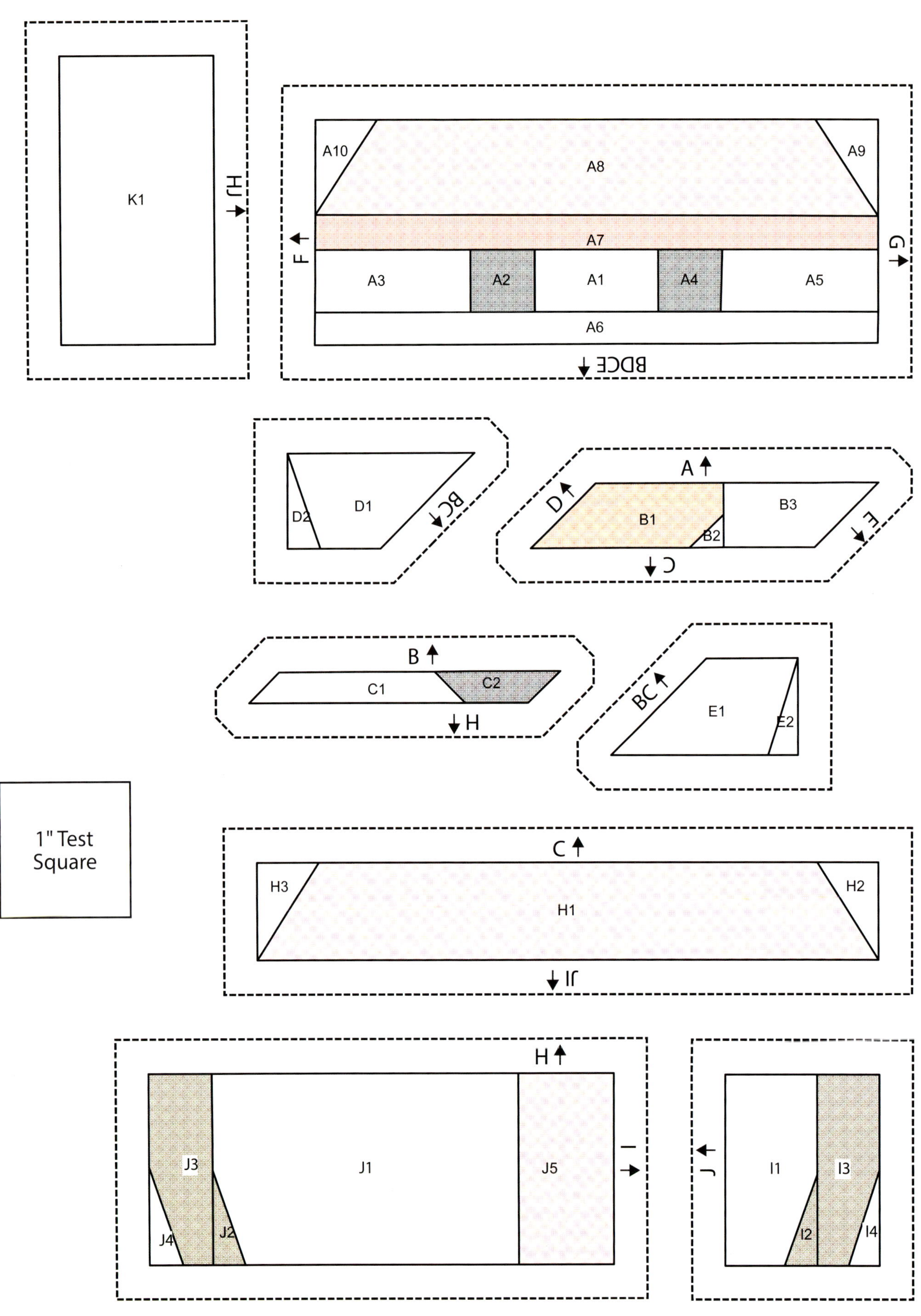

Happy Snowman, page 24

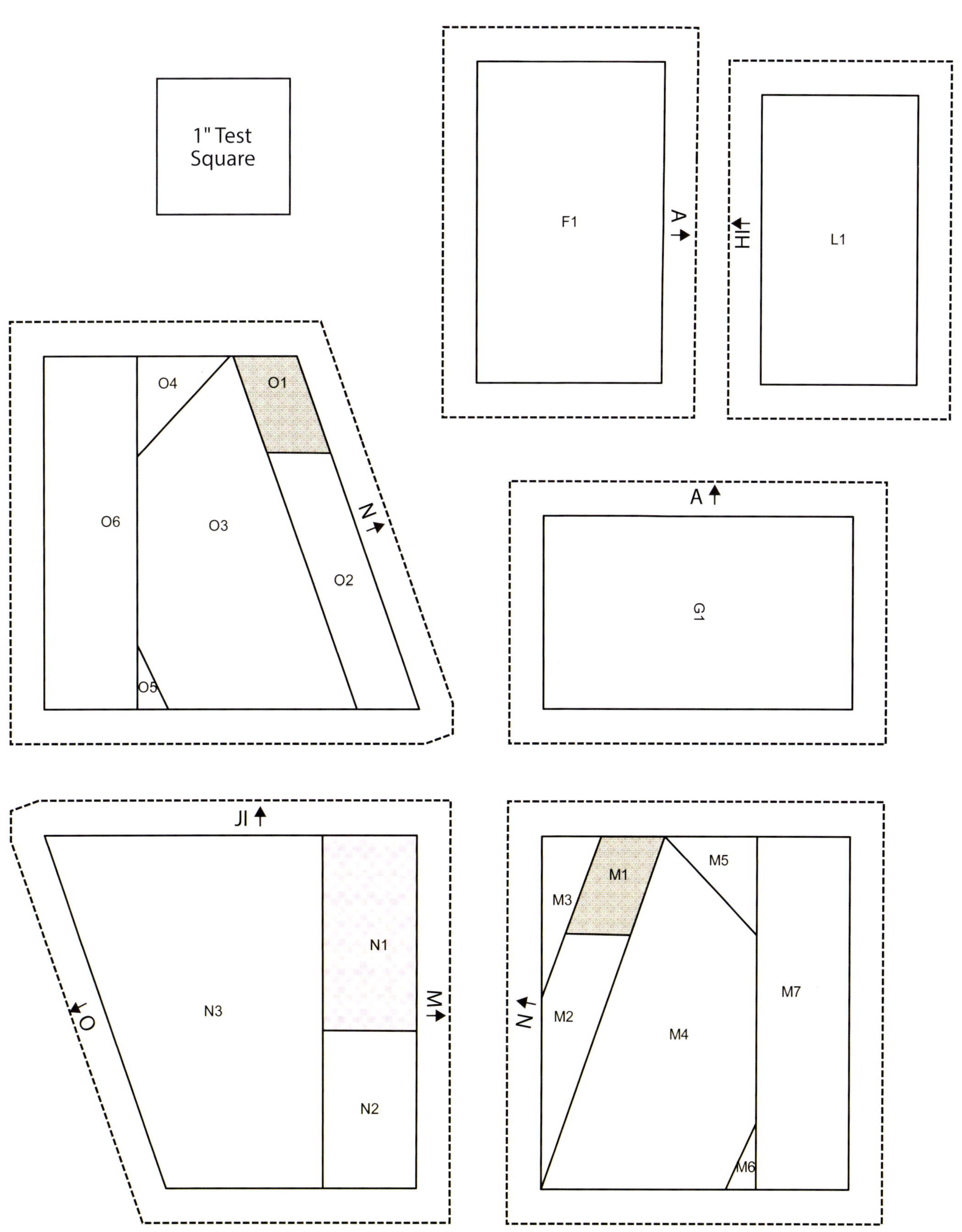

Happy Snowman, page 24

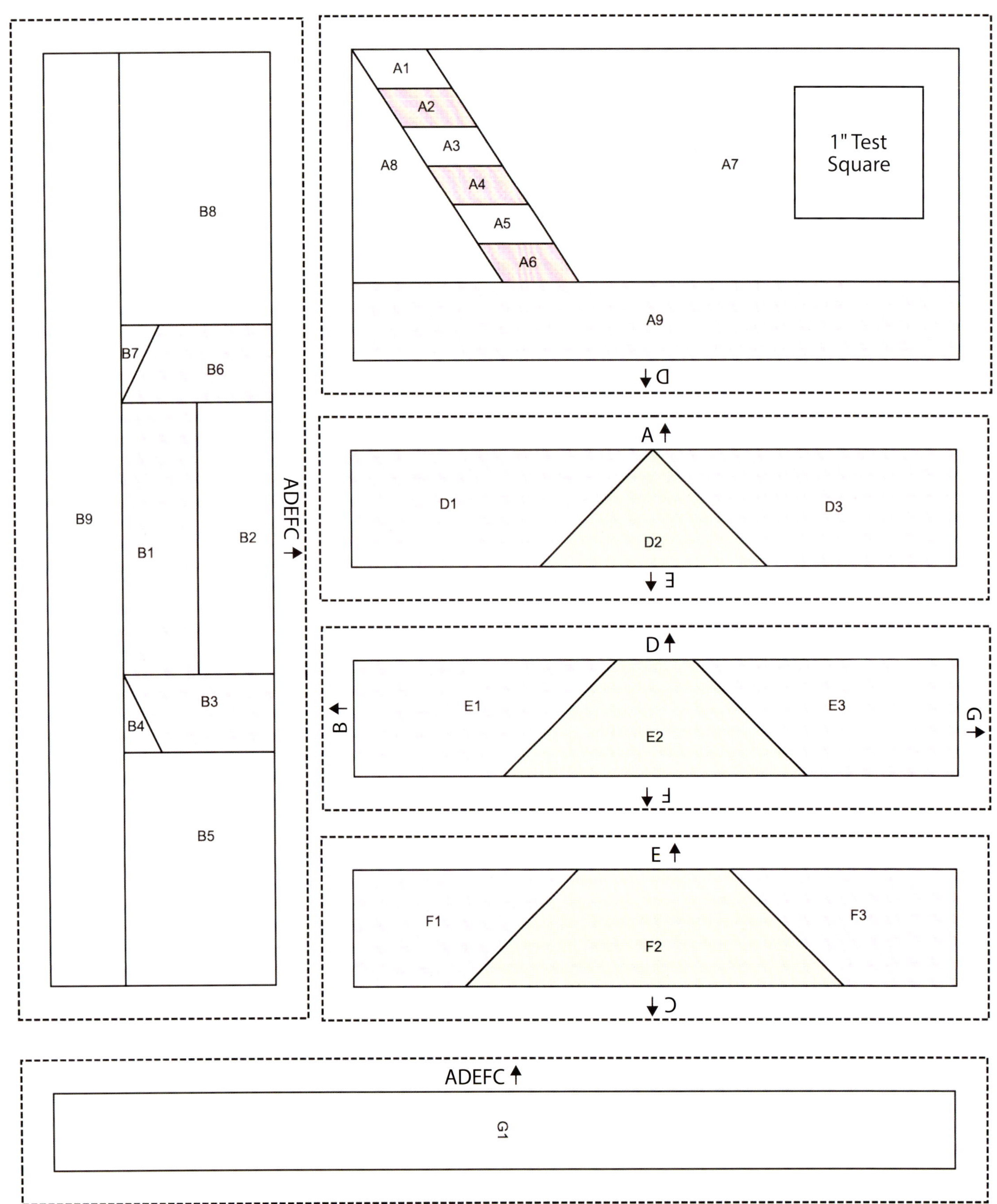

Hot Cocoa Mug, page 30

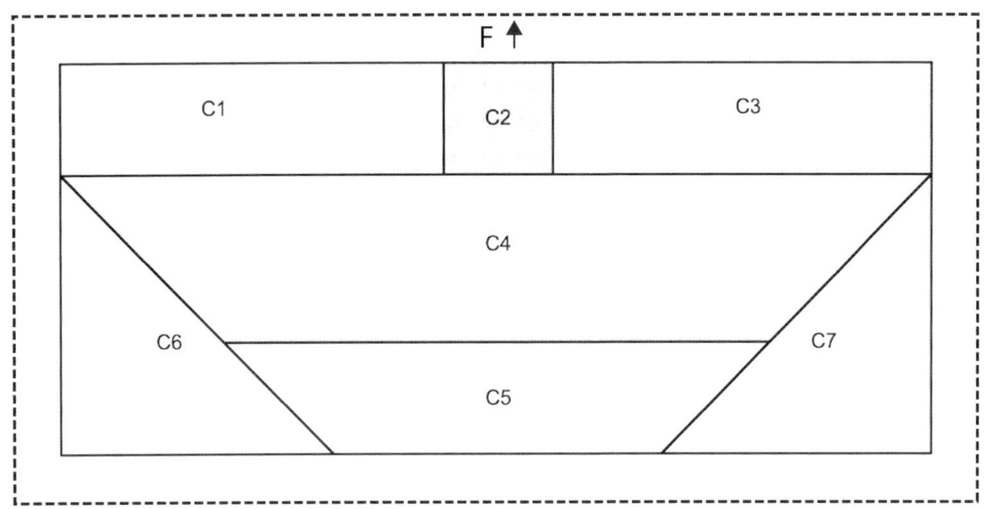

Hot Cocoa Mug, page 30

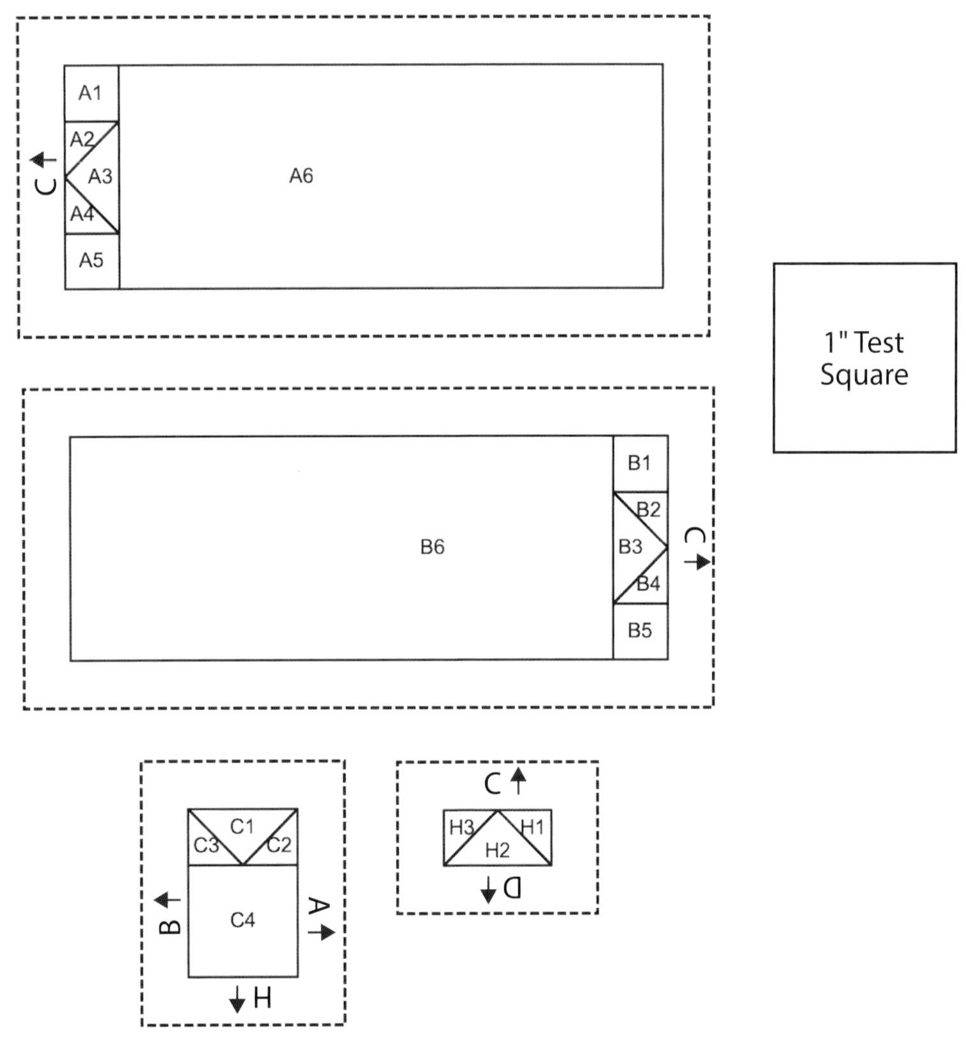

Christmas Tree, page 33

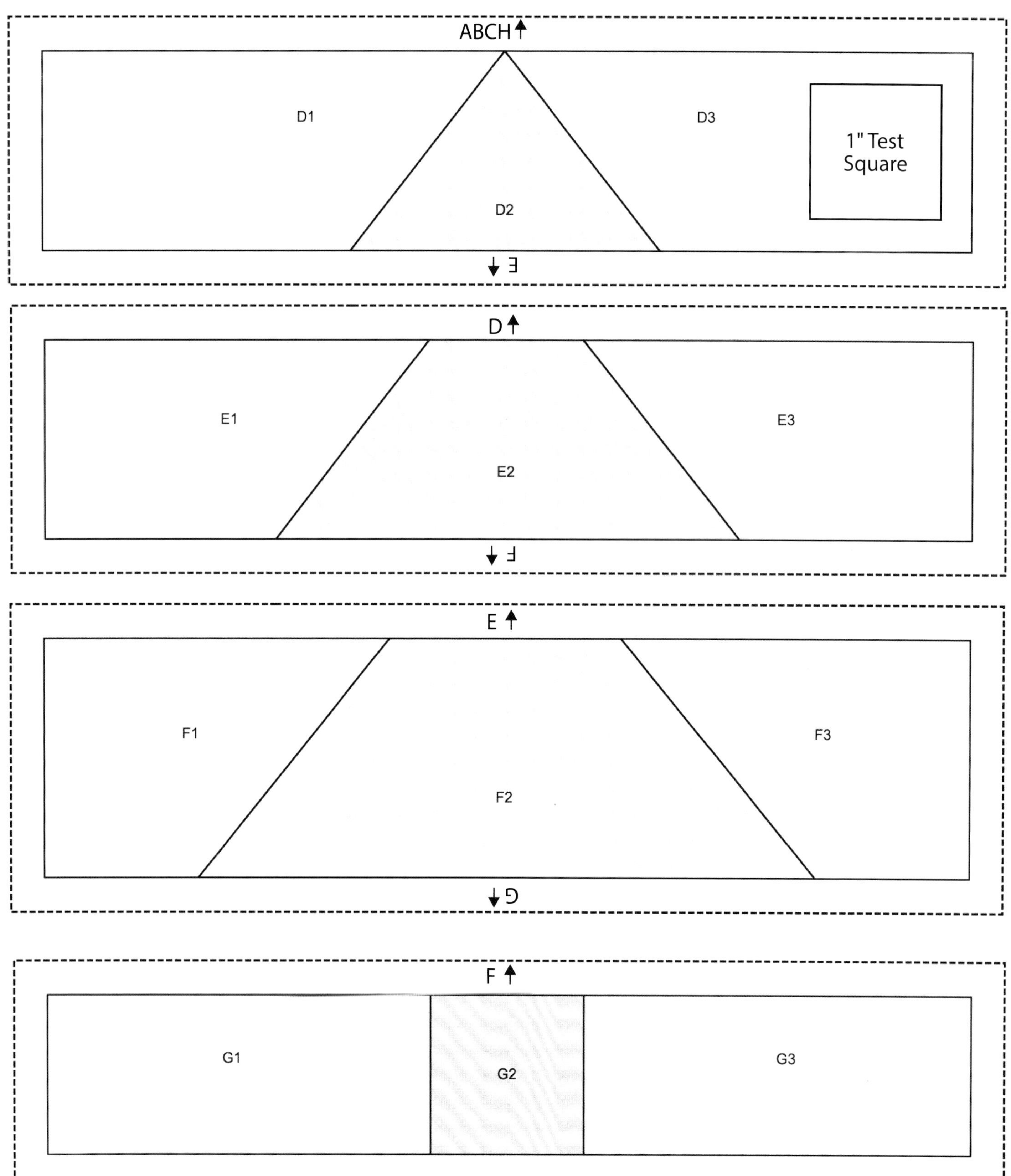

Christmas Tree, page 33

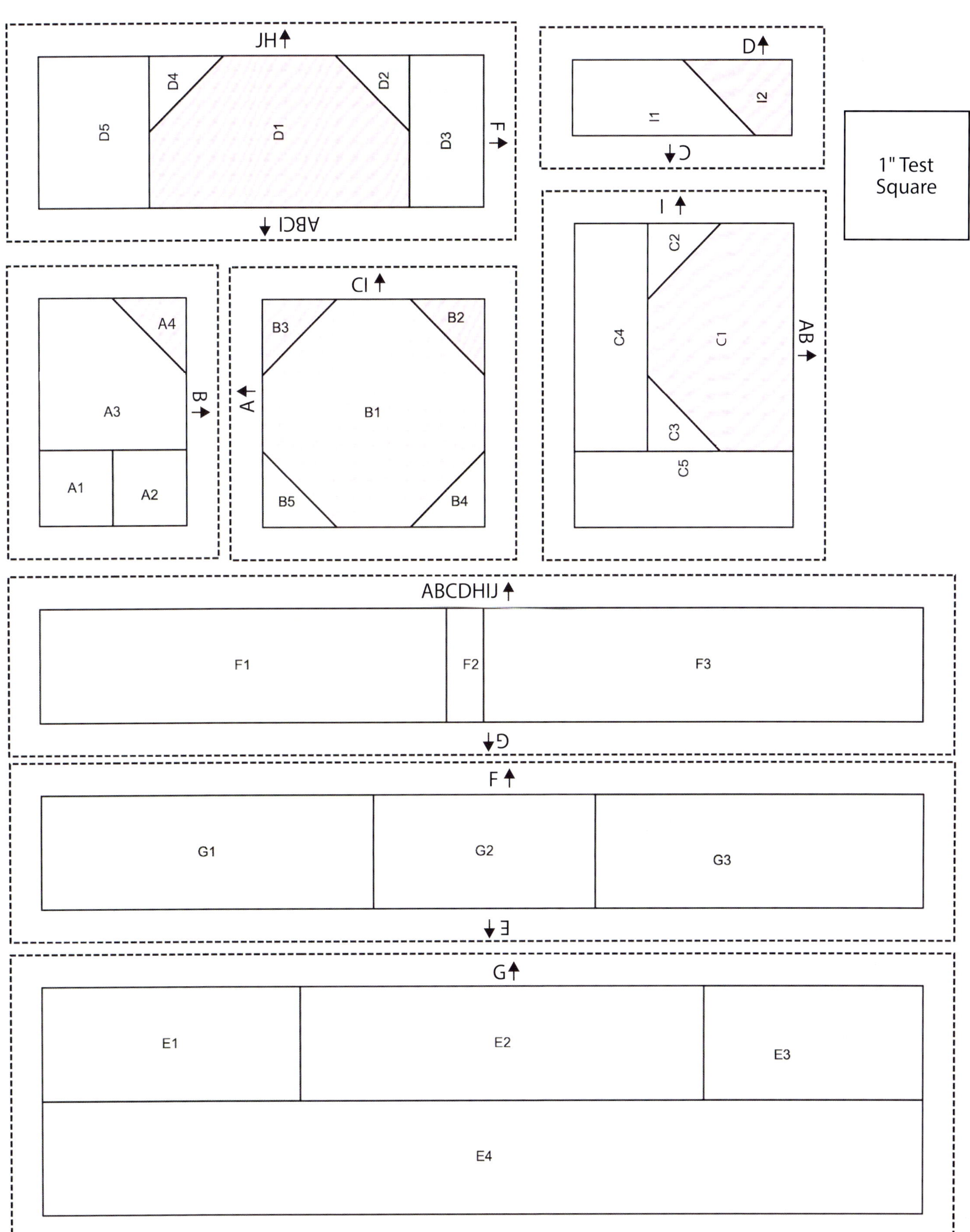

Holly Berries, page 39

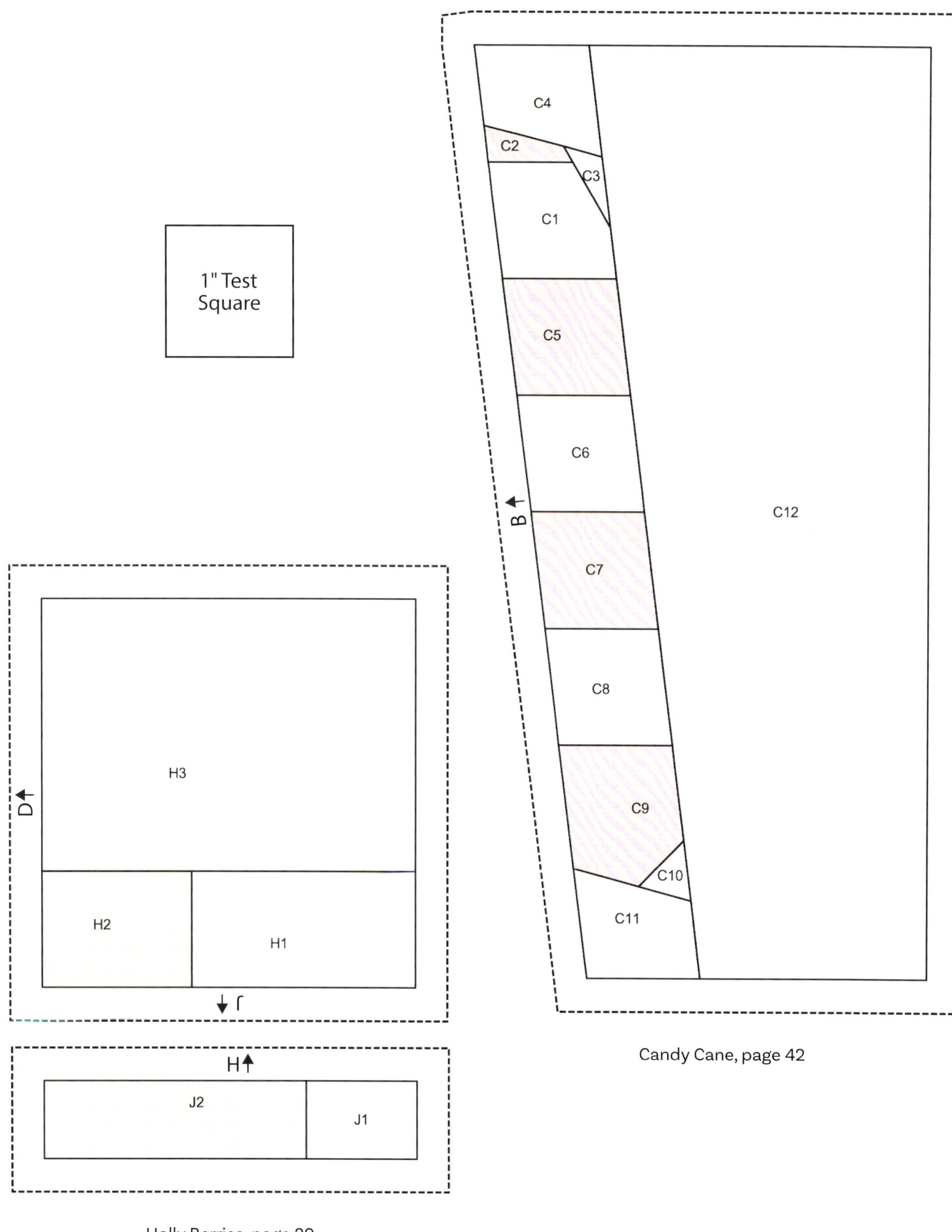

Candy Cane, page 42

Holly Berries, page 39

1" Test Square

B7
B6
B5
B4
B3
B2
B1
A4
A3
A2
A1
A5
A6
A7
A8
A9
B
A
C

Candy Cane, page 42

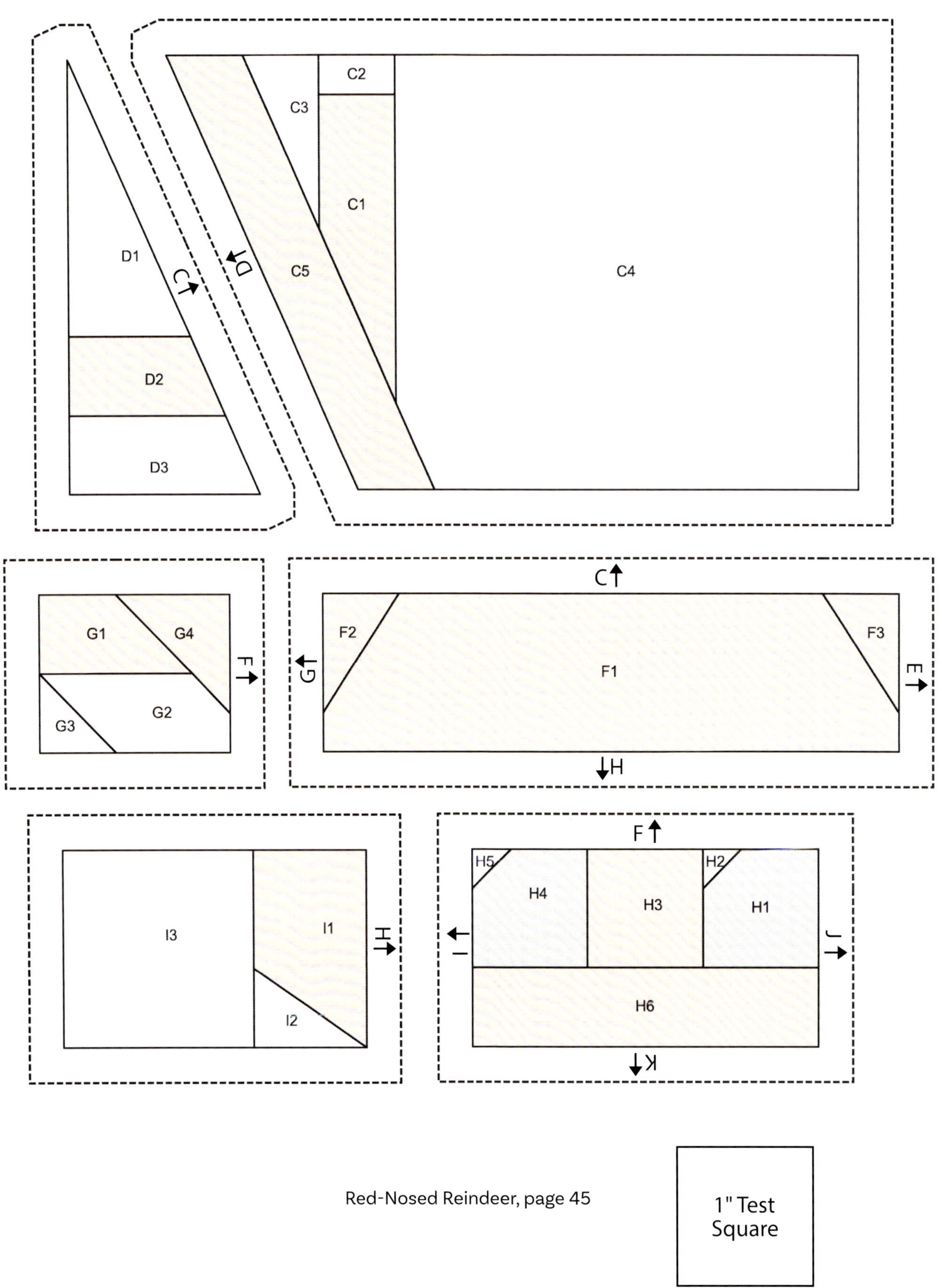

Red-Nosed Reindeer, page 45

1" Test
Square

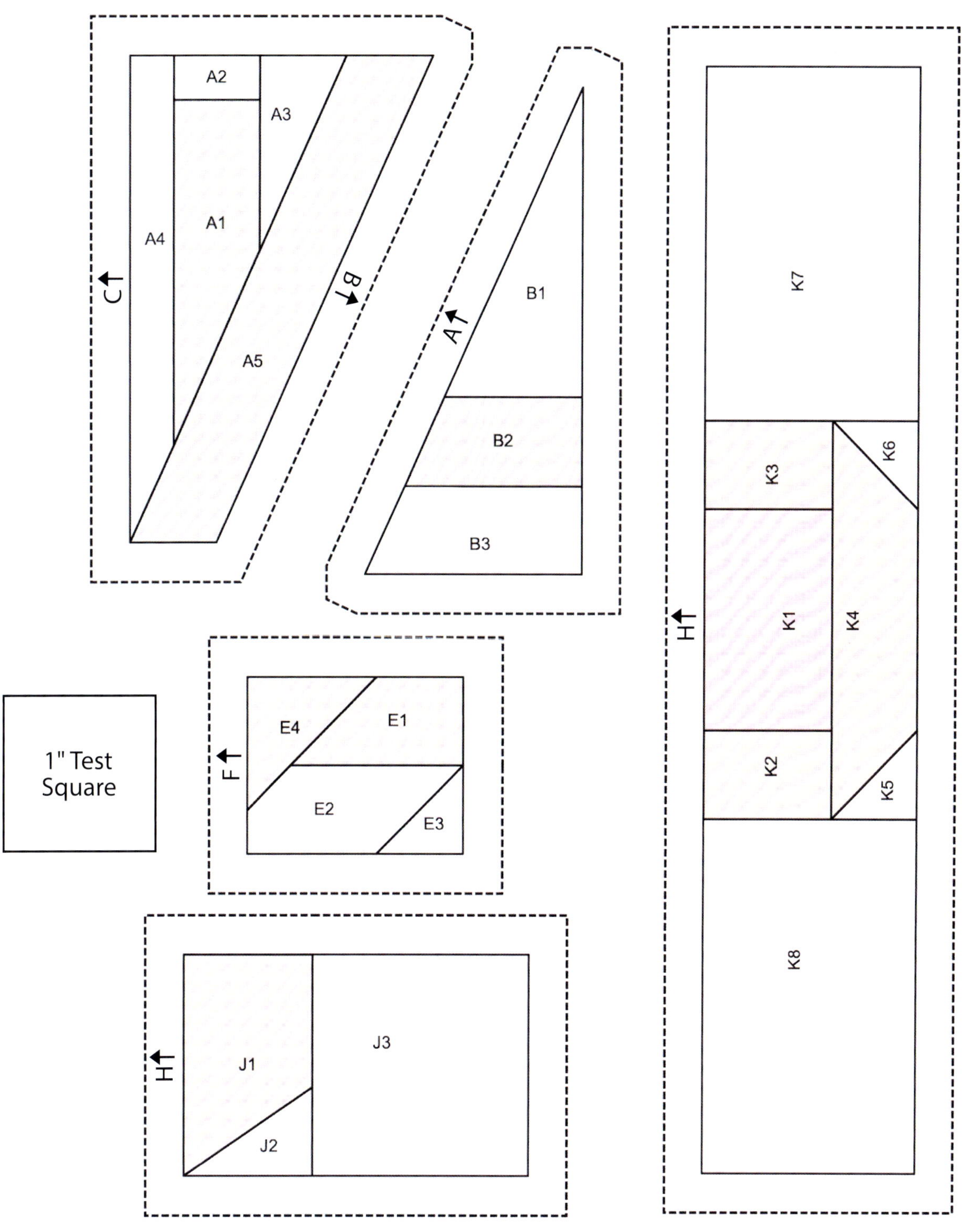

Red-Nosed Reindeer, page 45

L1

K

B7

B5

B2

B4

B1

B3

B6

IK

K1

K2

I

K

I4

B

A

I3

I2

I1

F

I

F3

F2

F1

F4

F5

D

F7

F6

E

F8

J

G4

G1

G2

G3

G5

D

D7

D1

D2

G

D6

D3

F

D4

D5

D8

F

J1

J3

J2

C

1" Test Square

Peppy Penguin, page 51

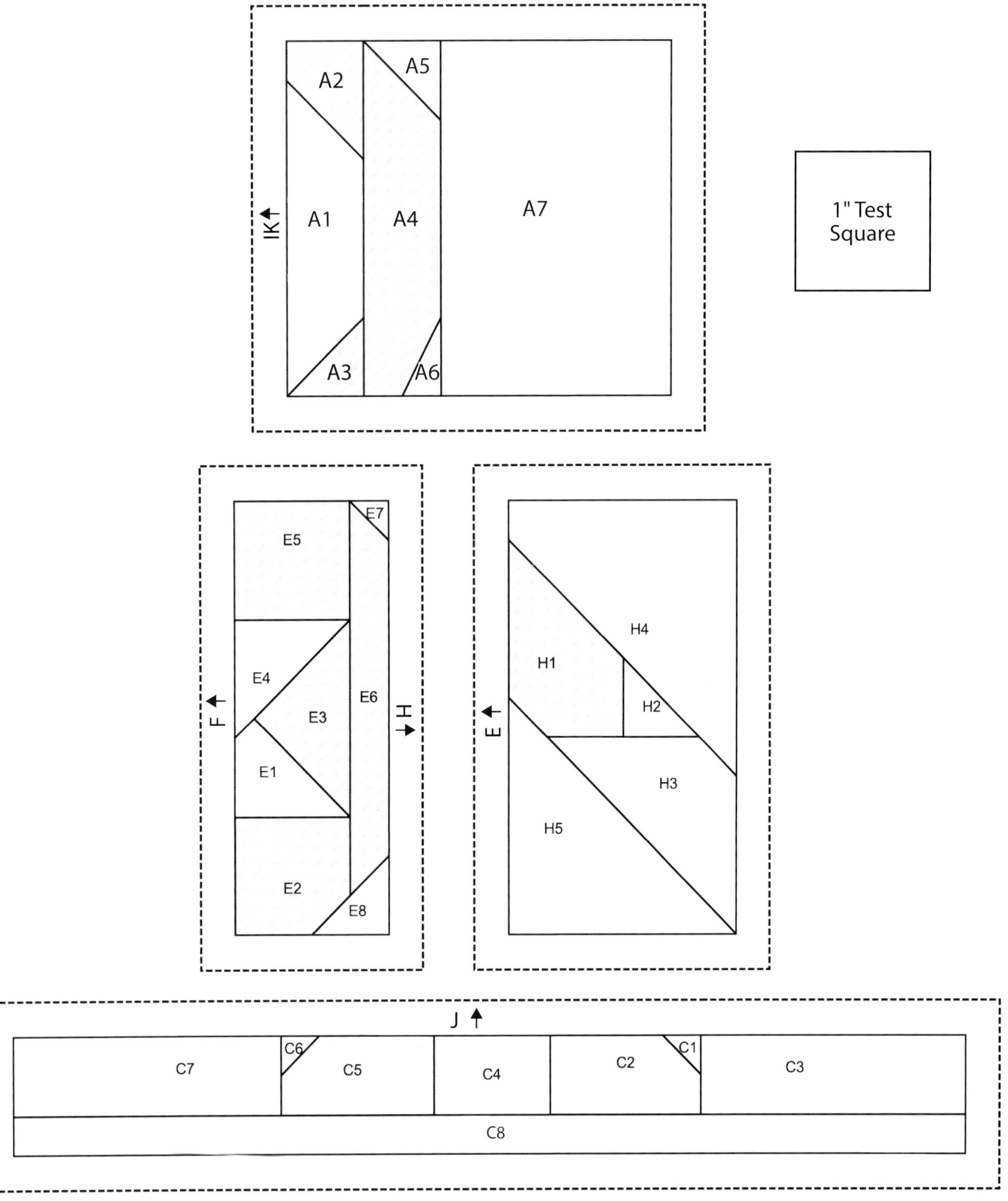

Peppy Penguin, page 51

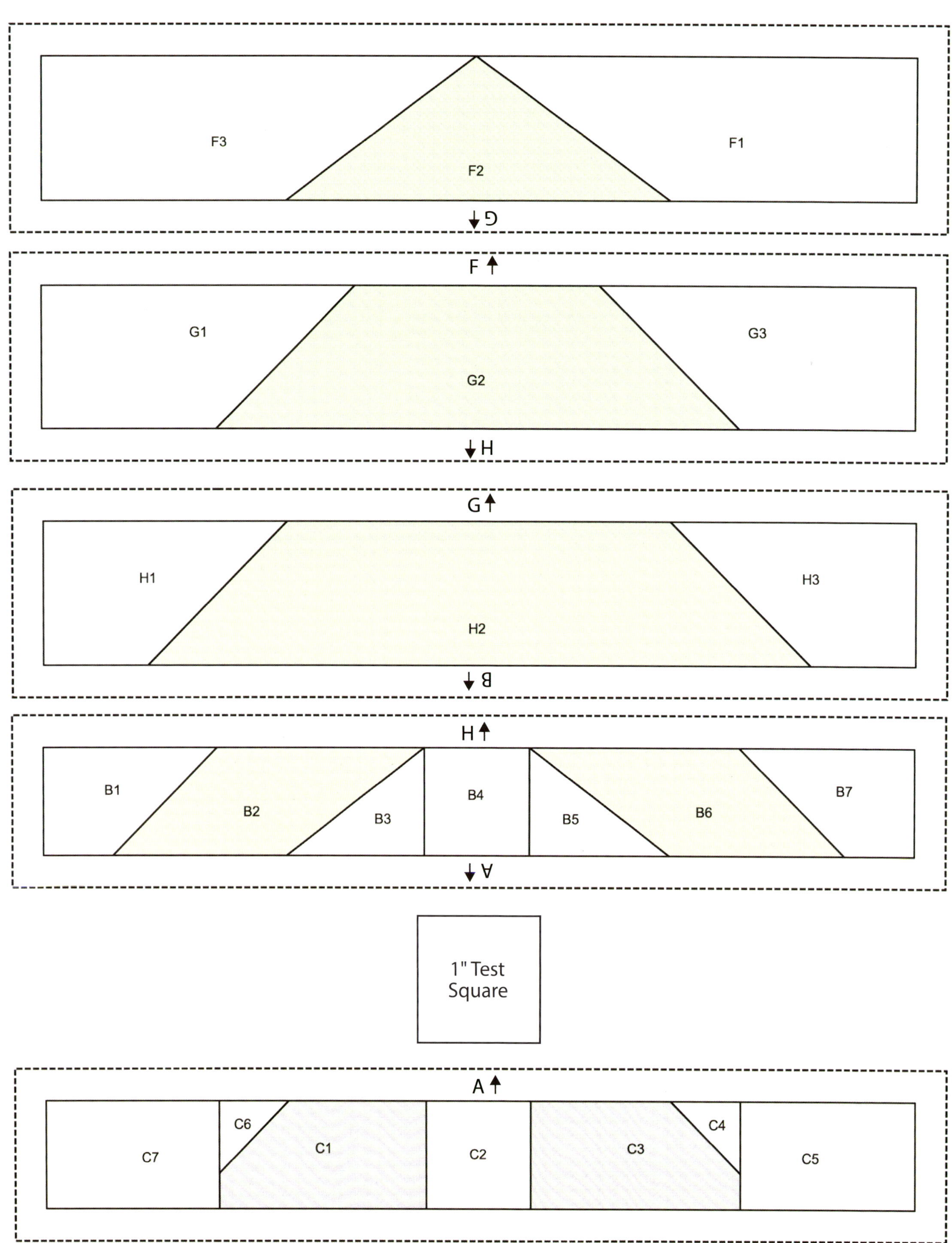

Jolly Gnome, page 58

1" Test Square

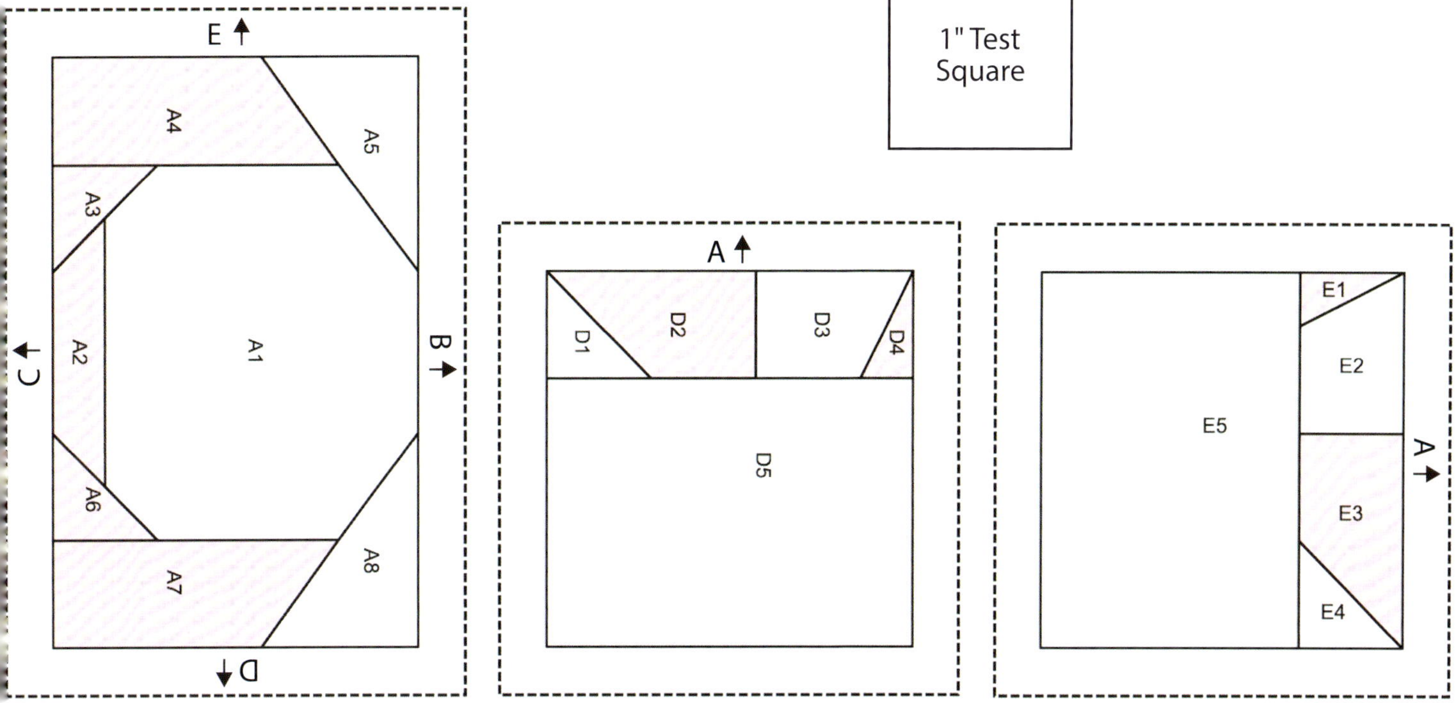

Jolly Gnome, page 58

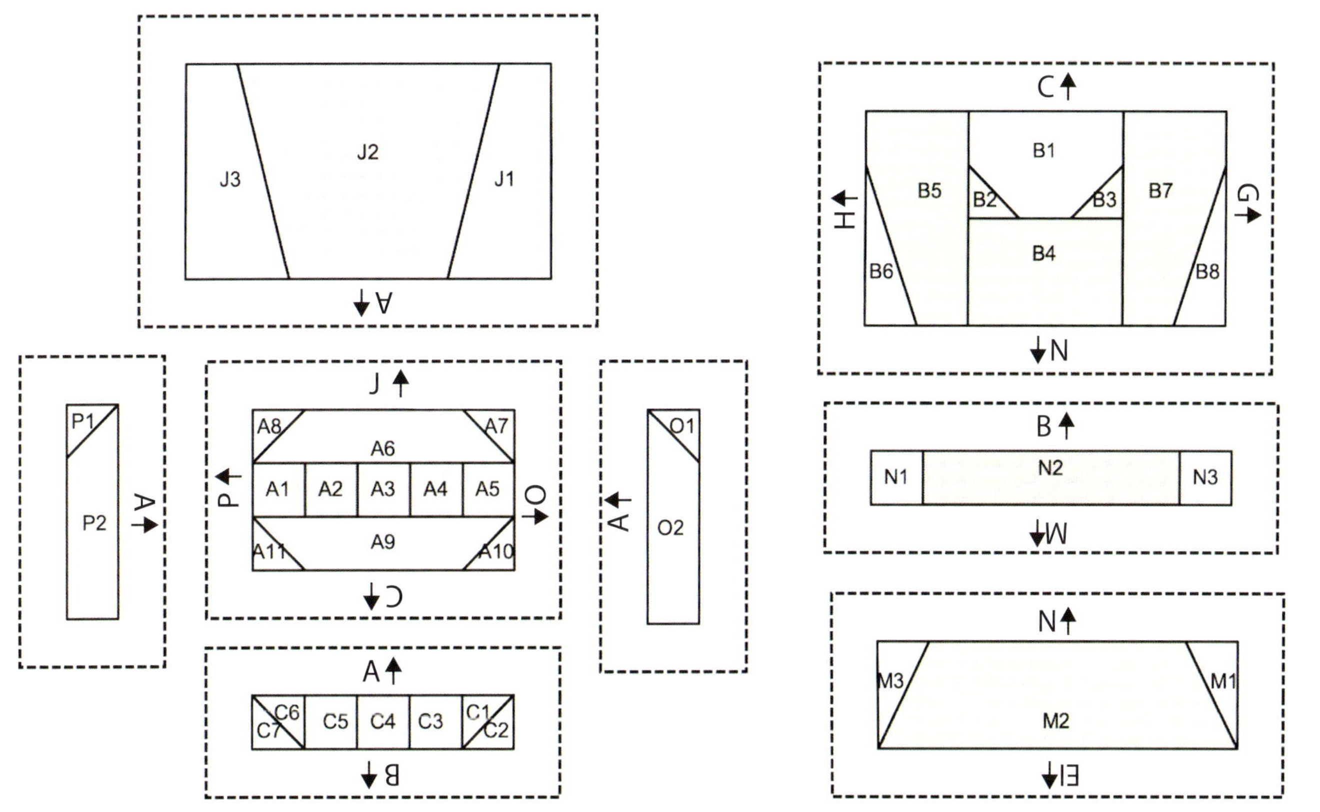

Nutcracker, page 54

Nutcracker, page 54

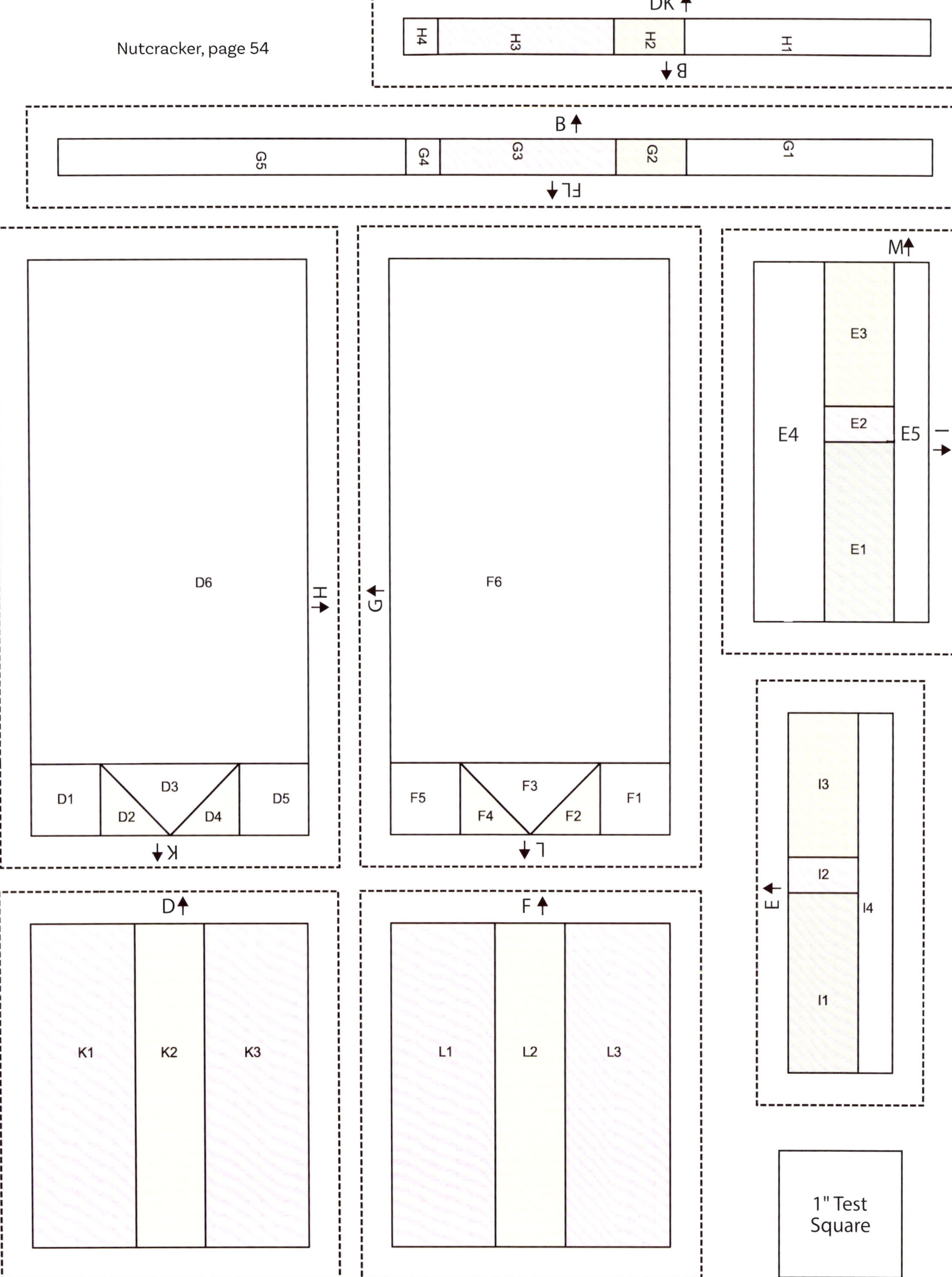

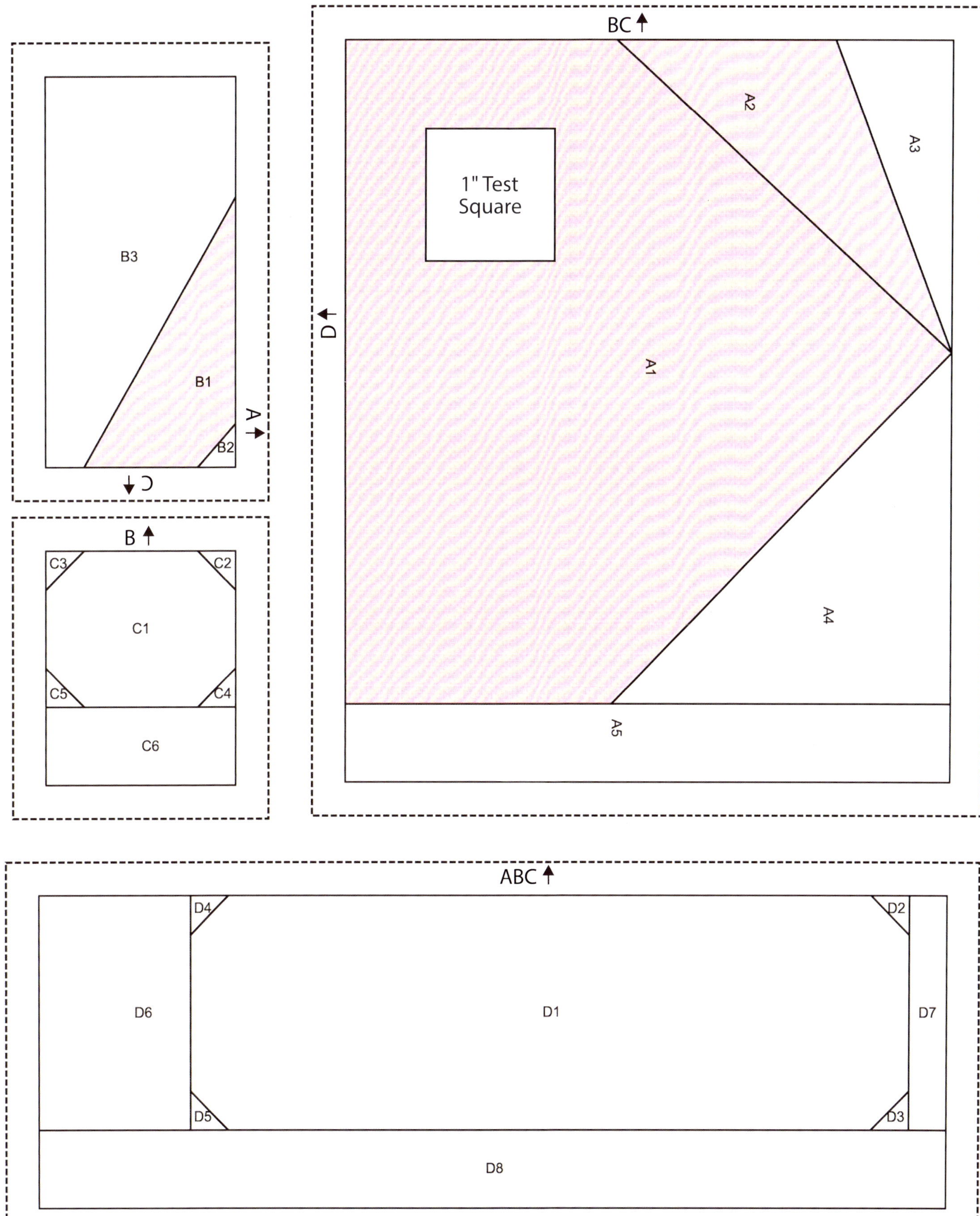

Santa Hat, page 36

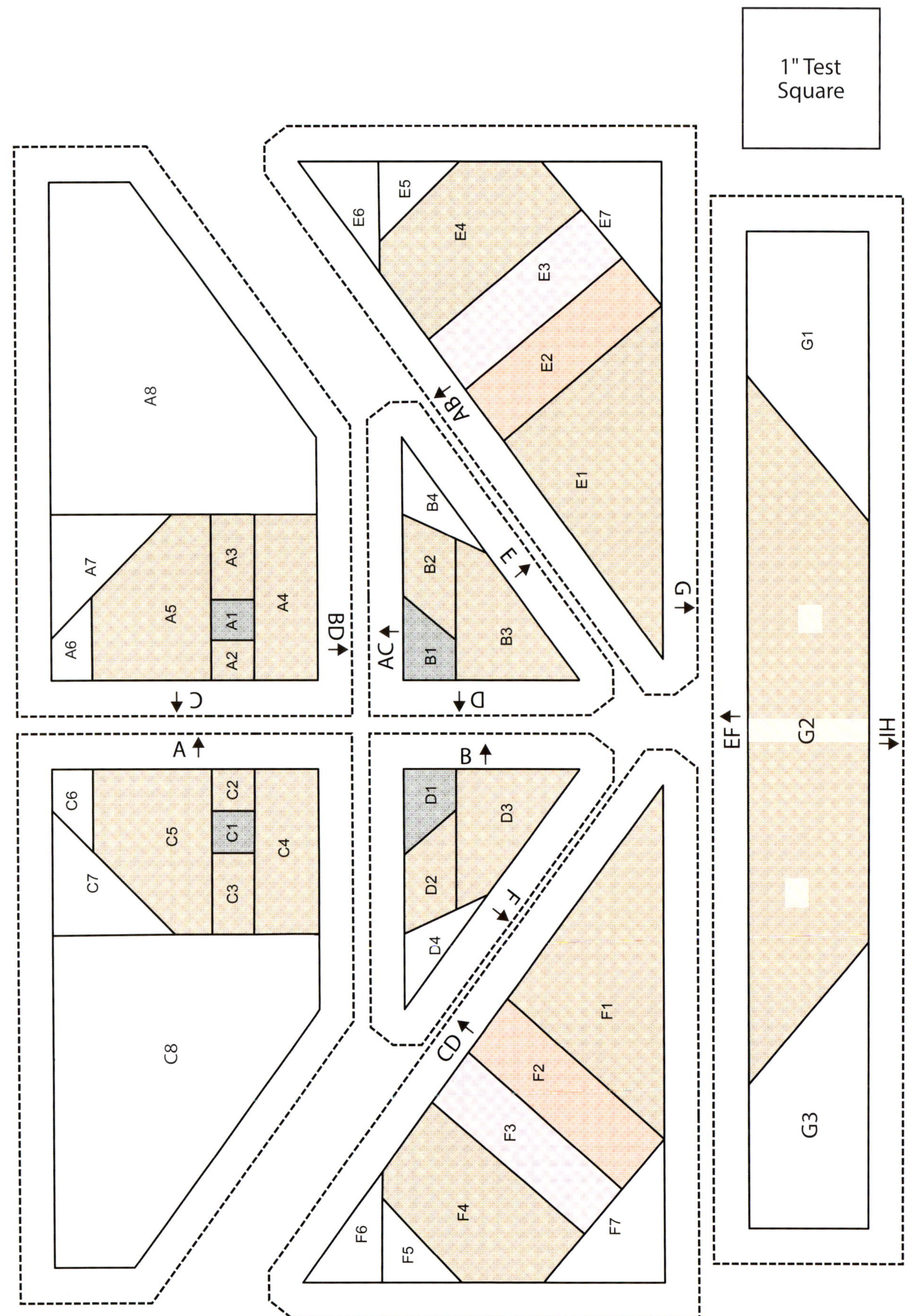

Gingerbread Man, page 48

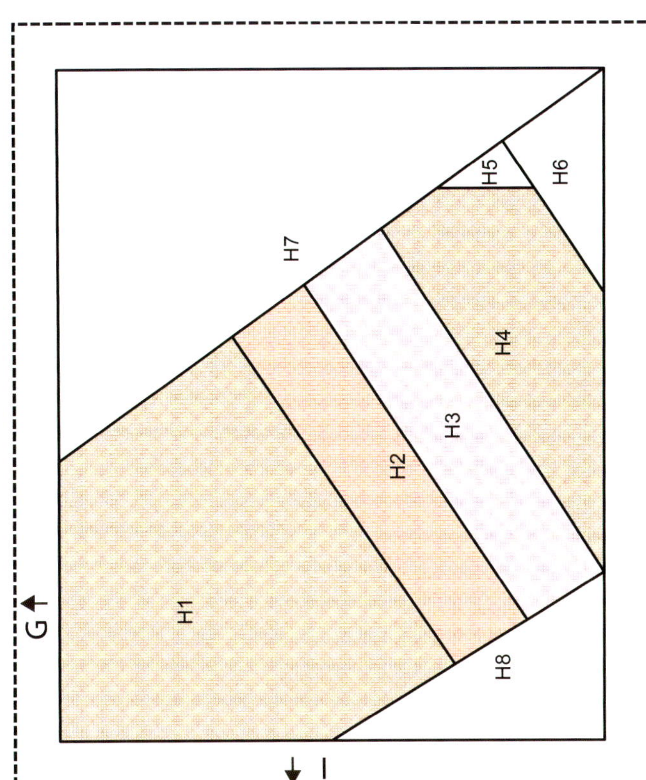

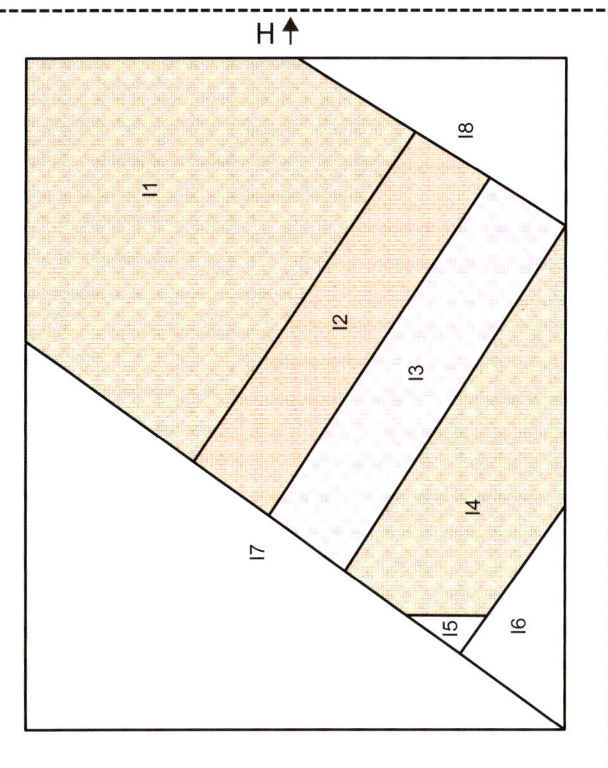

Gingerbread Man, page 48

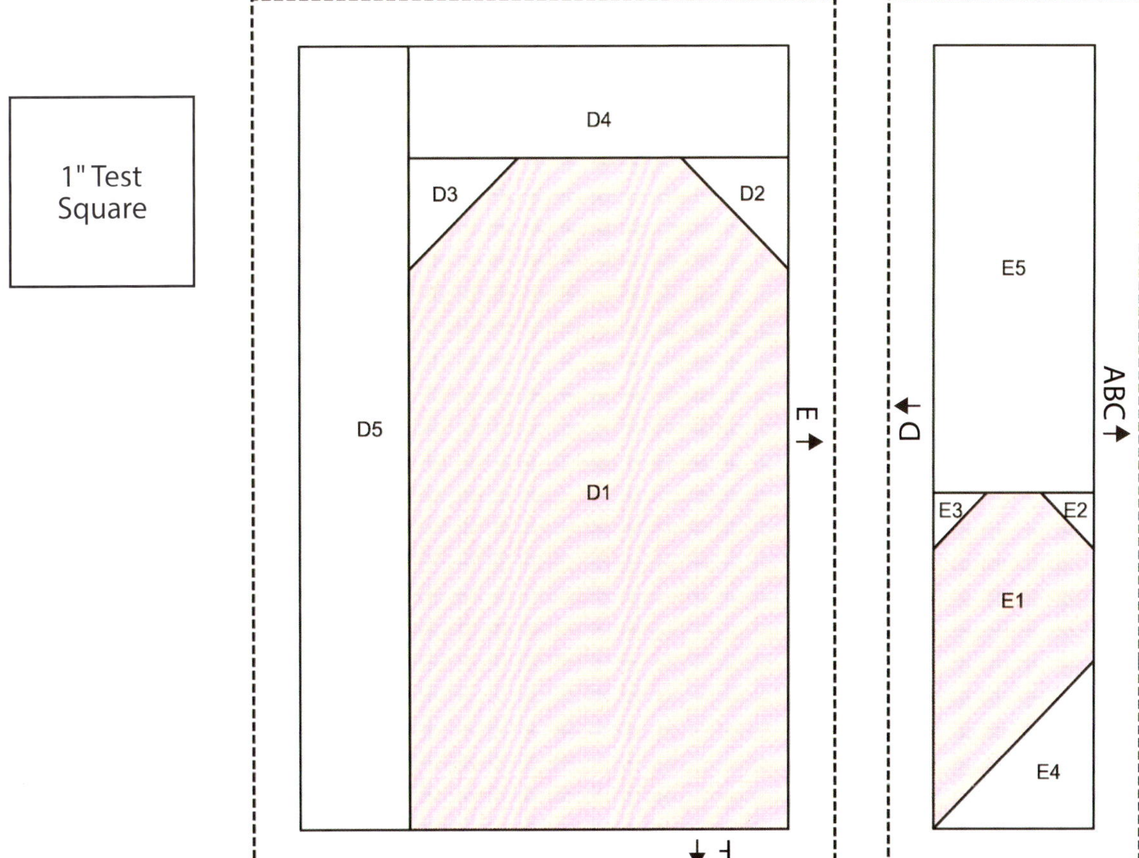

Cozy Mittens, page 27

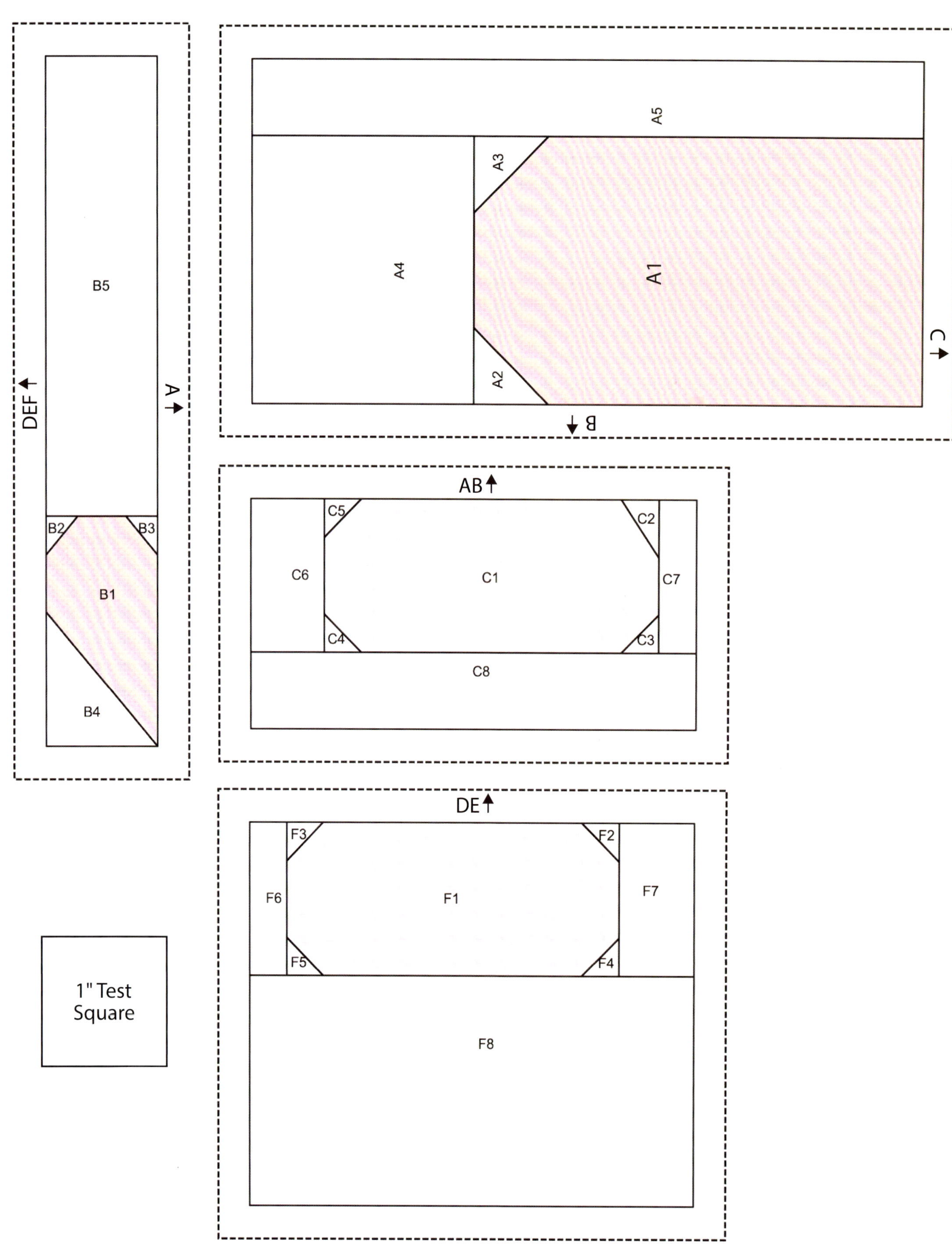

Cozy Mittens, page 27

Sewing Templates

Copy the following templates at 100%.
You can also download all the sewing pattern files at *foxpatterns.com/wonderful-world-christmas-blocks*.

Scan the QR code to quickly access the digital template page.

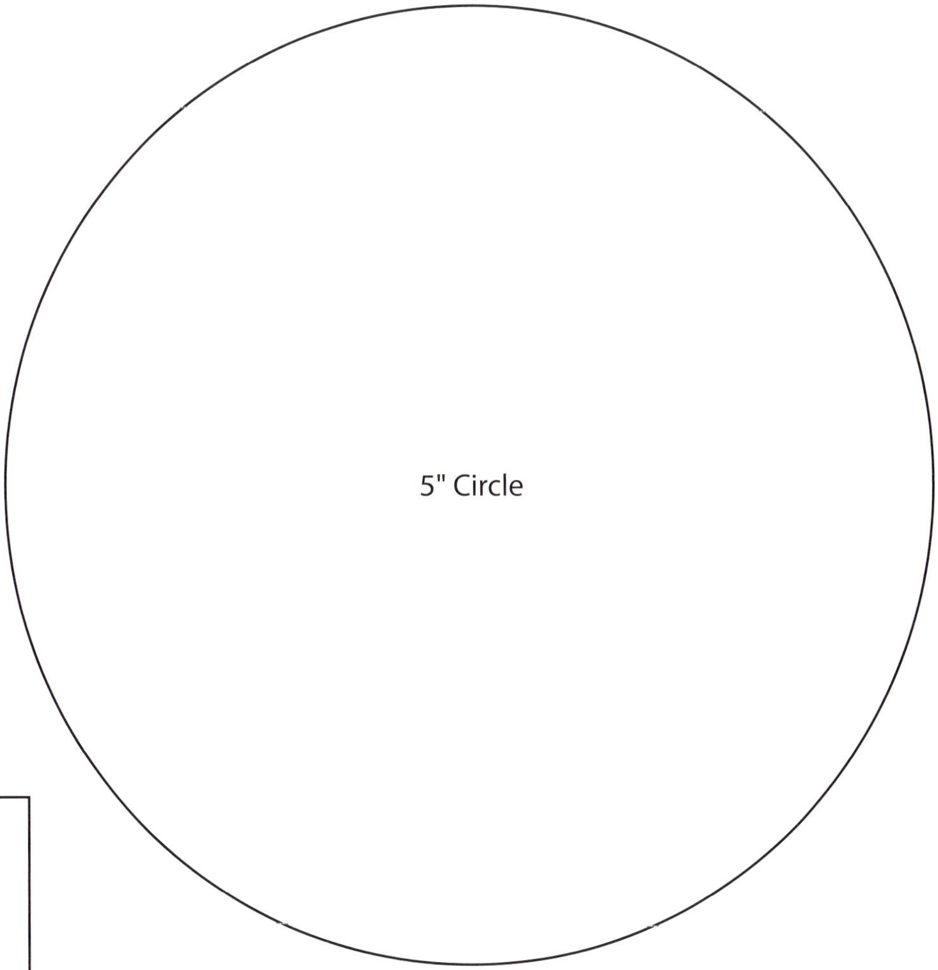

5" Circle

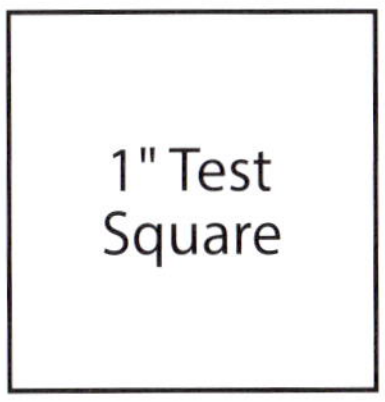

1" Test Square

Perfect Oven Mitts, page 87

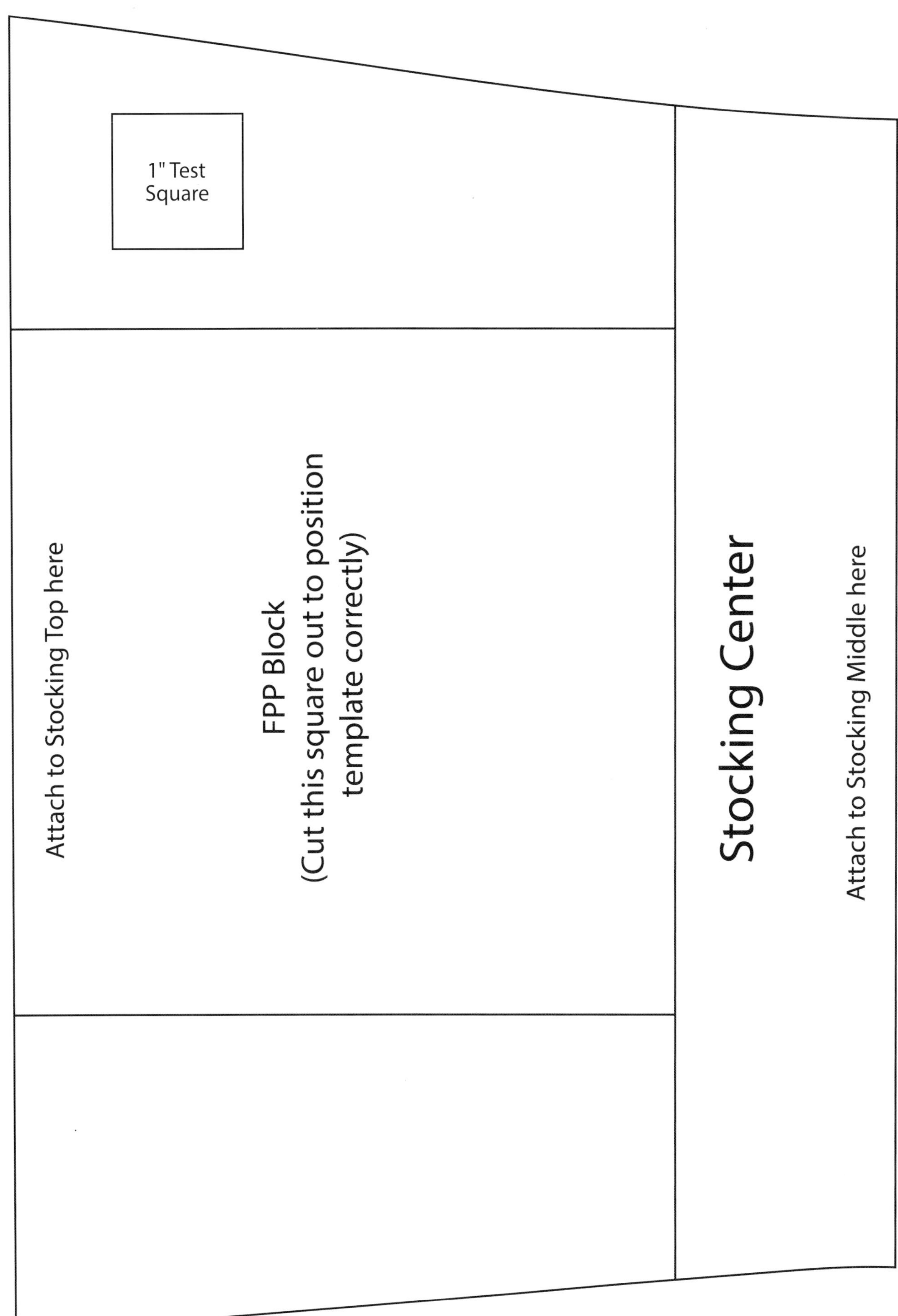

Cheerful Star Stocking,
page 66

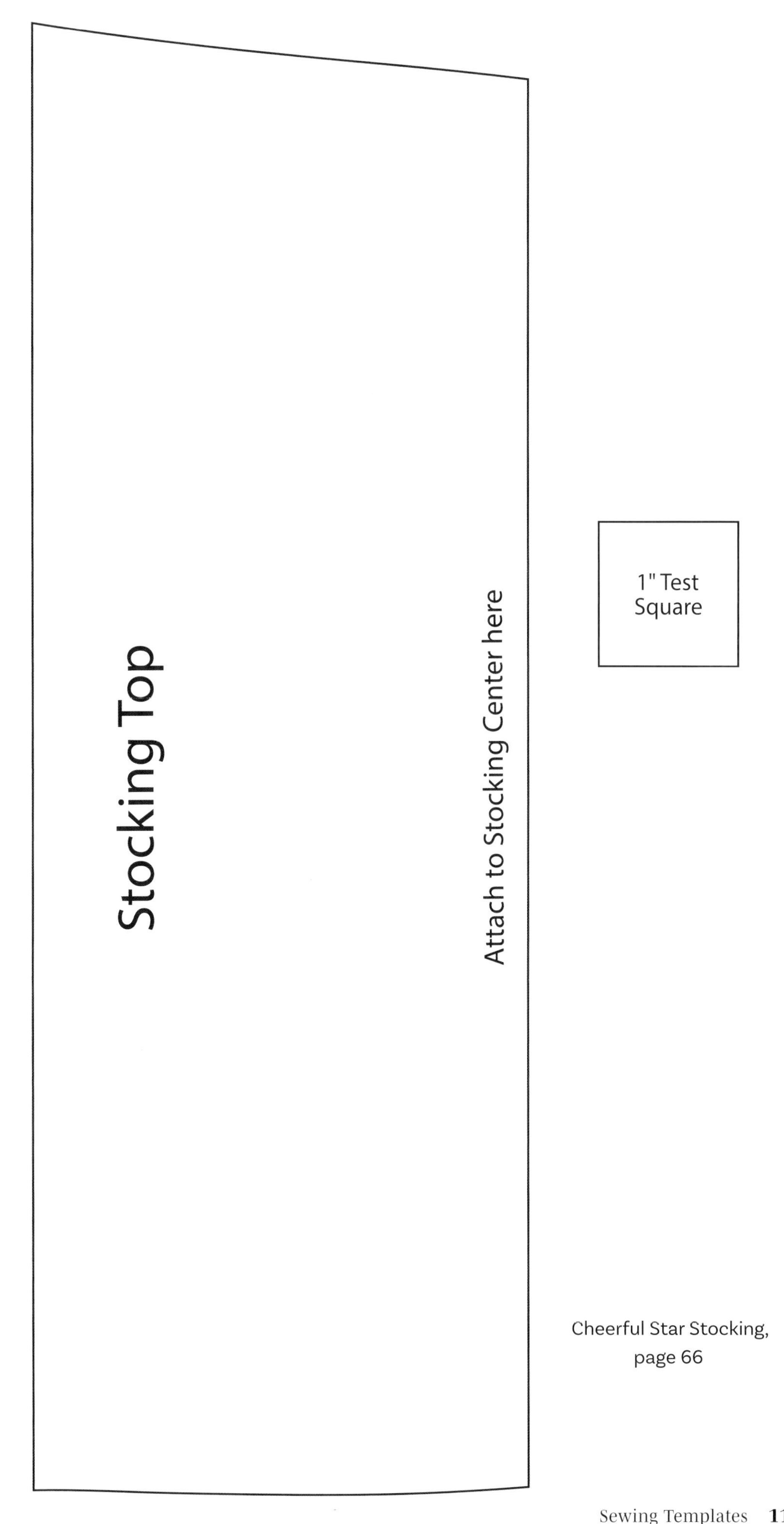

Cheerful Star Stocking, page 66

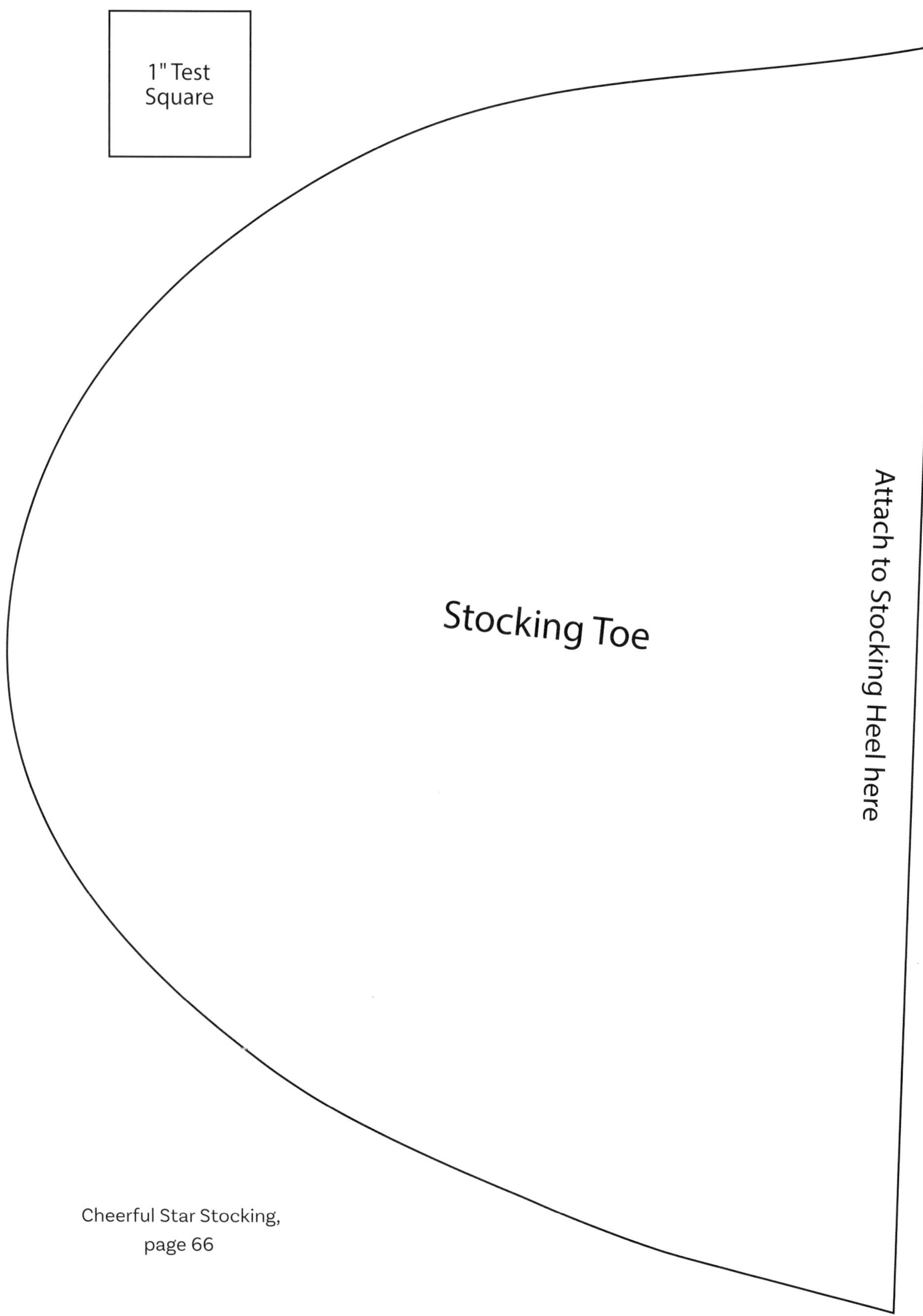

Cheerful Star Stocking,
page 66

Cheerful Star Stocking,
page 66

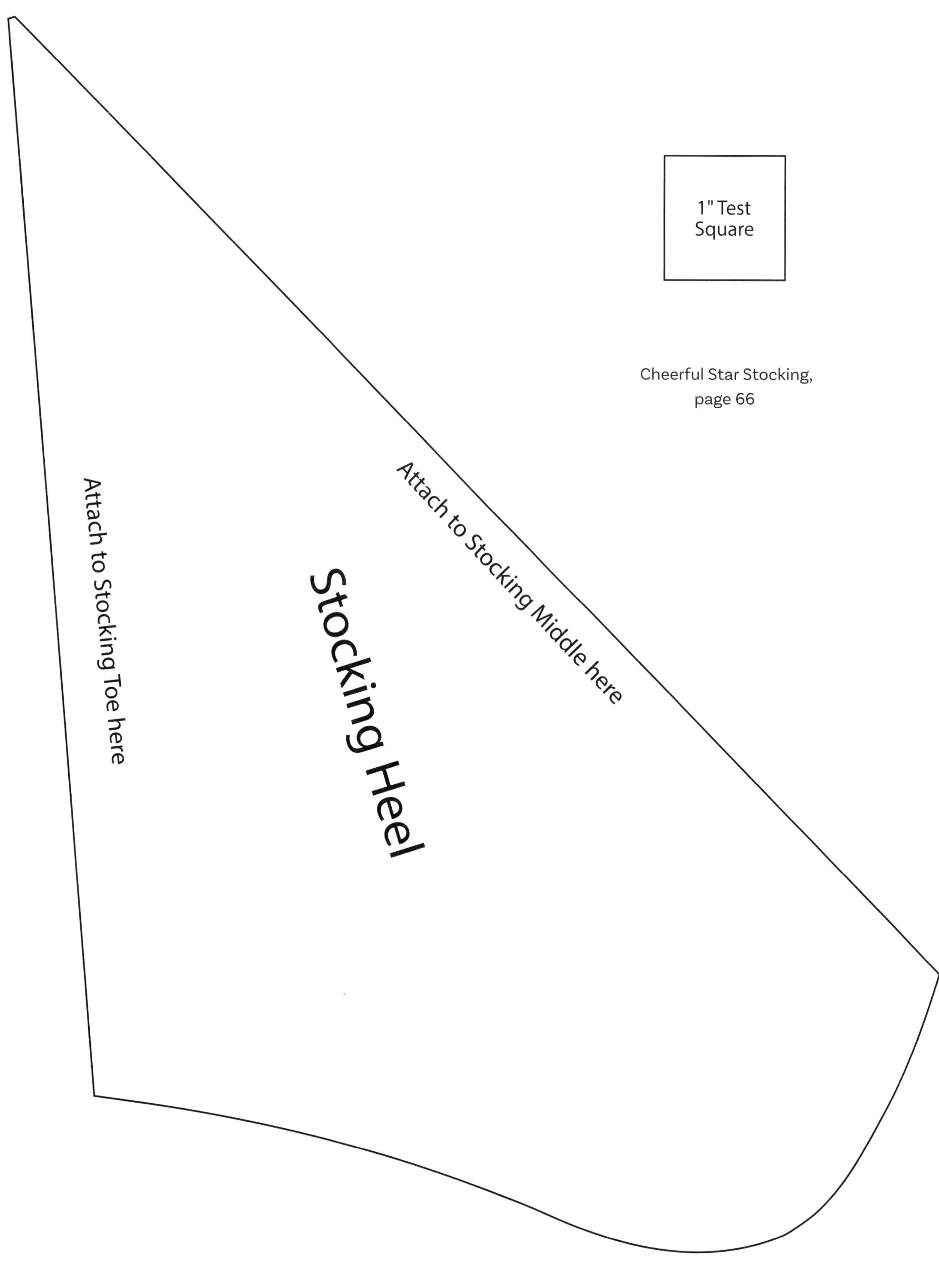
1" Test
Square
Cheerful Star Stocking,
page 66
Attach to Stocking Middle here
Stocking Heel
Attach to Stocking Toe here

Index

About the Author

Liza Taylor is a quilt pattern designer based in Salt Lake City, Utah, and a mom of two daughters. She began designing patterns in 2021 after having her first daughter, when she discovered how meaningful it was to create small, beautiful projects during her naps. Since then, she's fallen in love with foundation paper piecing and sharing it with others. Her passion is designing patterns that inspire people to pursue their creativity, slow down, and celebrate the joy of the handmade! See all that Liza creates on her social media *@lizataylorhandmade*.